THE PERSON AND WORK OF CHRIST

THE PERSON AND WORK OF CHRIST

Understanding Jesus

A.T.B. McGowan

Paternoster:
thinking faith

18 17 16 15 14 13 12   7 6 5 4 3 2 1

This edition first published 2012 by Paternoster
Paternoster is an imprint of Authentic Media Limited
Presley Way, Crownhill, Milton Keynes, MK8 0ES
www.authenticmedia.co.uk

British Library Cataloguing in Publication Data

A catalogue record for this book is available from the
British Library

ISBN: 978-1-78078-053-5

Cover design by David McNeil (revocreative)

To the Reverend Alexander Murray
Presbyterian minister and founding chairman of the
Highland Theological College, University of the
Highlands and Islands.
With deep gratitude for his support, encouragement,
patience and faith during the critical first fifteen years
of the life of the college.

Abbreviations

Contents

General Editor's Preface

Many books are written on the history of Christian doctrine, and volumes of systematic theology never cease to roll from the press. The former may or may not include reflections upon the current 'state of the doctrine'; the latter may or may not pay heed to the history of theological reflection upon the subject in hand. Hence this series entitled, *Christian Doctrines in Historical Perspective*, the objectives of which are twofold. First, to trace the biblical roots and defining moments in history of major Christian doctrines, with reference to prominent authors and texts (including recent ecumenical texts as appropriate), concluding with an appraisal of the doctrine in current debate. Secondly, to hold together doctrines which belong together but are sometimes, frequently for good reasons, treated in isolation from one another: for example, the Person *and* Work of Christ, Creation *and* Re-creation.

Authors have been commissioned to write scholarly works of interest to a readership comprising senior undergraduates and above.

It is hoped that this series will contribute to that biblical-historical grounding of current theological reflection which is necessary if systematic and constructive theology are to be understood as the product of a conversation between the biblical sources, the heritage of doctrinal thought and the current intellectual environment.

Alan P. F. Sell
Milton Keynes, U.K.

Acknowledgements

Thanks to my editor, Mike Parsons, for his patience. Thanks too for allowing me, without abandoning the commission I was given by Alan Sell (as indicated in his General Editor's Preface), to try and write the book in a way that would be accessible not only to students and academics but also to others prepared to think seriously about the Christian faith. This reflects my own transition from principal of Highland Theological College to parish minister, during the writing of the book. It also reflects my conviction that every Christian should try to read and understand as much as possible about the Bible and Christian theology.

Thanks to Dr Jason Maston of Highland Theological College and to the Rev. Dr Malcolm Maclean of Greyfriars Free Church in Inverness, for reading and commenting upon the first draft of this manuscript. Their comments were invaluable and very much appreciated.

Thanks to my congregation at Inverness East Church of Scotland and to my secretary Dolina Coventry. Thanks particularly to the elders, for their willingness to allow me to continue my writing and academic interests alongside my preaching and pastoral work. It was while preaching a series of sermons on the person and work of Christ that I decided to make the transition from a purely academic book to one from which members of my congregation might benefit. The sermons can be heard at http://www.invernesseast.com/resources/sermons.

Thanks to IVP for allowing me to use, at various places in the book, sections from my chapter 'Affirming Chalcedon' in *The Forgotten Christ* (ed. Stephen Clark; Nottingham: IVP, 2007), pp. 19–47. Also my chapter 'The Atonement as Penal Substitution' in *Always Reforming: Explorations in Systematic Theology* (ed. A.T.B. McGowan; Leicester: Apollos, 2006), pp. 183–210.

All quotations are from the New International Version of the Bible (UK edition).

Finally, thanks to my wife June for all her love and support. Her willingness to live with a husband who is either out visiting his congregation, or living in his study, is remarkable!

1

Introduction

In this book, we are going to consider the person and work of Christ. In theological language, we are going to study Christology, which deals with the person of Christ, and the atonement, which deals with the work of Christ. When we are considering the person of Christ, we are asking about his identity, about his humanity and his divinity, about where he fits into the Trinity as well as all the issues relating to his becoming a human being at a certain point in history. When we are considering the work of Christ, we are asking what he accomplished by his death and resurrection but also through his perfect life of obedience and by his continuing work of intercession. It should be stressed, however, that this division into person and work is purely for the purpose of study and analysis since the Christ we encounter in Scripture is united in being and act.

Four points regarding this book ought to be stressed at the beginning. First, it is written in the conviction that our understanding of Christology and atonement must, like all our other doctrines, be drawn from Scripture. The presupposition on which this book is based is that the canonical Scriptures of the Old and New Testaments (the sixty-six books which together make up the Bible) have been 'breathed out' by God (2 Timothy 3:16), written by men who were 'carried along by the Holy Spirit' (2 Peter 1:21) and therefore they are the infallible Word of God. God continues to speak through these Scriptures by his Holy Spirit and, as the 'Word of God written', they constitute the final authority on all matters of faith and conduct.

Second, the writer of this book is a minister of the Church of Scotland and a theologian in the Calvinist tradition. This means that the book has been written from the perspective of the 'Reformed' tradition within Christianity. For the first thousand years of its existence the church was united, although with a number of separate 'provinces'. In the eleventh century a great divide opened up in the church between the Eastern,

Greek-speaking Church (later called Eastern Orthodox) and the
Western, Latin-speaking Church (later called Roman Catholic).
Following the Reformation, there was another great divide opened up
between Roman Catholicism and Protestantism. There then followed
another divide within Protestantism, creating three strands of thinking:
Lutheran, Reformed and Anabaptist. There have been many further
divisions since, to our shame and cost. It should be said that, although
this book is written from the 'Reformed' or 'Calvinist' perspective, the
author is critical of his own tradition at a number of points and also
believes in the importance of dialogue with other traditions.

Third, this book is a contribution to the field of systematic and historical theology and so considerable time will be spent on the development in understanding, within the life of the Christian church, of
the various aspects of the doctrines of the person and work of Christ.
To this end, each chapter (or group of chapters where there is too
much material for one chapter) will follow the same pattern. We shall
begin by laying out the biblical teaching on the subject under discussion and this will be followed by a description and analysis of the way
in which this teaching was subsequently received, reflected upon and
understood by the church. This order is both chronological (Scripture
came first; theological reflection came later) and theological (Scripture
must take priority over the church's theological dogma). Particular
attention will be given to major advances in Christian theology and
also to the various heresies. The heresies are important for two reasons: first, because they were often the catalyst which forced the
church to come to a common mind on a subject; and second, because
some of these heresies continue to appear in various forms in the
churches.

Fourth, in writing this book there is a recognition that theology did
not end with the great councils of the early centuries or with the
Reformation, nor even with the post-Reformation confessional codifi-
cation of doctrine and that there is much work still to be done. As we
shall see, although the church came to a general agreement on the
doctrine of the person of Christ, it did not do so in relation to the work
of Christ. That is unfinished business.

Who is Jesus of Nazareth?

In order to introduce this study, we are going to focus on the identity
of Jesus of Nazareth. In around AD 27, when a Jew called Jesus began

to draw a circle of disciples around himself, he might easily have been mistaken for just another wandering rabbi. It soon became apparent, however, that this man was out of the ordinary. Before long he had achieved a significant following, not least because of the simplicity and the power of his teaching about the kingdom of God. Indeed, such was his growing reputation that he came to the attention of the Jewish religious leaders. The problem for them was that he was not part of the Jewish establishment, had not trained at one of the rabbinical schools and yet he was challenging their authority and their teaching.

In addition to this, stories were circulating which suggested that this man was a prophet sent from God. Some had heard that his mother was a virgin at the time he was born; others said that they had heard God speak when Jesus was being baptized in the river Jordan by John the Baptist. All of this attention was further intensified when Jesus began to heal the sick. Crowds of people began to follow him wherever he went. Then others claimed that he had walked on water and that he had fed five thousand people with a few loaves and some fish. It was even said that he had raised people from the dead.

The key question which had to be answered concerned his identity. Was he simply a rabbi who told a good story and could hold the attention of a crowd, or was he really a miracle worker? Was he a prophet in the Jewish mould or simply a troublemaker, trying to make a name for himself at the expense of the Jewish leaders? More troubling still, was he a political agitator, who was likely to bring the wrath of the Roman authorities down on the Jews?

As we read the four gospels, our primary sources of information about the life of Jesus, it is the 'identity' question which surfaces again and again. Again and again the question comes in different forms: Who are you? By what authority are you doing these things? When he went back to his home town it was the same:

> When the Sabbath came, he began to teach in the synagogue, and many who heard him were amazed. 'Where did this man get these things?' they asked. 'What's this wisdom that has been given him, that he even does miracles! Isn't this the carpenter? Isn't this Mary's son and the brother of James, Joseph, Judas and Simon? Aren't his sisters here with us?' And they took offence at him (Mark 6:2–3).

At the end of Jesus' life when he was on trial, the high priest asked him, 'Are you the Christ, the Son of the Blessed One?' (Mark 14:61).

Even his own disciples had cause to ask the question after the calming of the storm: 'Who is this? Even the wind and the waves obey him!' (Mark 4:41).

In Matthew 16:13–17, Jesus raises the question of his own identity and asks his disciples a question:

> When Jesus came to the region of Caesarea Philippi, he asked his disciples, 'Who do people say the Son of Man is?' They replied, 'Some say John the Baptist; others say Elijah; and still others, Jeremiah or one of the prophets.' 'But what about you?' he asked. 'Who do you say I am?' Simon Peter answered, 'You are the Christ, the Son of the living God.' Jesus replied, 'Blessed are you, Simon son of Jonah, for this was not revealed to you by man, but by my Father in heaven.'

Here we see some of the rumours that were circulating concerning his identity. These suggestions were not surprising, given the Jewish understanding of the Scriptures. There is a prophecy in Malachi 4:5 about Elijah coming before the Messiah. These Jews thought it meant literally that Elijah would return from the dead. The proper interpretation of the Malachi passage was that someone would come 'in the spirit and power of Elijah' as we see from Luke 1:17 and in that sense the prophecy was fulfilled in the coming of John the Baptist, as Jesus himself explained in Matthew 17:12. There was also a prophecy in Deuteronomy 18:15–18 about the coming of another prophet like Moses, which did actually refer to the Messiah, as we're told in Acts 3:22 and 7:37.

Jesus is the Christ

When Jesus asks his disciples their own view concerning his identity, it is Peter who speaks for the group. The first part of Peter's answer ('You are the Christ') is deeply rooted in the Jewish understanding of the Scriptures because, for over 800 years, the Jews had been expecting God to send Messiah. When we speak about Jesus of Nazareth, we often use the name 'Jesus Christ'. It is important to remember, however, that 'Christ' was not his surname; it is a title which means 'Messiah' ('Christ' is the Greek word used in the New Testament to translate the Hebrew word 'Messiah'). It would probably be more accurate to say 'Jesus the Christ' or 'Jesus the Messiah'. Let's consider what 'Christ' or 'Messiah' means.

The Anointed One

The word 'Messiah' means 'God's anointed'. In the Old Testament there were three offices to which men were appointed by anointing (either literally or symbolically). First, there was the prophet. In Isaiah 61:1 the prophet makes this declaration: 'The Spirit of the Sovereign LORD is on me, because the LORD has anointed me to preach good news to the poor.' Second, there was the priest. If you remember the story of how Moses consecrated Aaron and the other priests, you will know that they were anointed. As we read in Leviticus 8:30, 'Then Moses took some of the anointing oil and some of the blood from the altar and sprinkled them on Aaron and his garments and on his sons and their garments. So he consecrated Aaron and his garments and his sons and their garments.' Then third, there was the king. When God told Samuel that Saul had been rejected by God and that a new king was to be appointed, he was led to the house where David lived. After considering his brothers, we are told in 1 Samuel 16:12–13 that Samuel 'sent and had [David] brought in. He was ruddy, with a fine appearance and handsome features. Then the LORD said, "Rise and anoint him; he is the one." So Samuel took the horn of oil and anointed him in the presence of his brothers, and from that day on the Spirit of the LORD came upon David in power.'

When Jesus came as the Messiah he was anointed by God. This is what Peter said in Acts 10:37–38: 'You know what has happened throughout Judea, beginning in Galilee after the baptism that John preached – how God anointed Jesus of Nazareth with the Holy Spirit and power, and how he went around doing good and healing all who were under the power of the devil, because God was with him.' The writer to the Hebrews says something similar in Hebrews 1:8–9. Comparing Jesus to the angels he says: 'But about the Son he says, "Your throne, O God, will last for ever and ever, and righteousness will be the sceptre of your kingdom. You have loved righteousness and hated wickedness; therefore God, your God, has set you above your companions by anointing you with the oil of joy."'

If we ask which of the 'anointed offices' Jesus fulfilled, we discover something very remarkable. As the Messiah, he was fulfilling all three of the offices which required anointing. In other words, he was Prophet, Priest and King. John Calvin used this threefold office to explain who Jesus is and what he accomplished.[1]

---

[1] John Calvin, *Institutes of the Christian Religion*, 2/15/1–6, Library of Christian Classics (ed. J.T. McNeill; Philadelphia: Westminster, 1977), vol. 1, pp. 494–503.

Prophet

The prophet is one who speaks on behalf of someone else. We see this in Exodus 7:1–2: 'Then the LORD said to Moses, "See, I have made you like God to Pharaoh, and your brother Aaron will be your prophet. You are to say everything I command you, and your brother Aaron is to tell Pharaoh to let the Israelites go out of his country."' Then in Deuteronomy 18:18–22 God lays down guidelines for recognizing a true prophet:

> I will raise up for them a prophet like you from among their brothers; I will put my words in his mouth, and he will tell them everything I command him. If anyone does not listen to my words that the prophet speaks in my name, I myself will call him to account. But a prophet who presumes to speak in my name anything I have not commanded him to say, or a prophet who speaks in the name of other gods, must be put to death. You may say to yourselves, 'How can we know when a message has not been spoken by the LORD?' If what a prophet proclaims in the name of the LORD does not take place or come true, that is a message the LORD has not spoken. That prophet has spoken presumptuously. Do not be afraid of him.

Bruce Milne put it like this: 'His office presupposes people's ignorance and blindness with respect to God's will and purpose which the prophet as spokesman of the Almighty seeks to dispel.'[2] A prophet, then, is someone who speaks to the people on behalf of God.

The early Christians believed that Jesus was a prophet. As we read in Matthew 21:45–46, 'When the chief priests and the Pharisees heard Jesus' parables, they knew he was talking about them. They looked for a way to arrest him, but they were afraid of the crowd because the people held that he was a prophet.' Or again in Luke 7:11–17:

> Soon afterwards, Jesus went to a town called Nain, and his disciples and a large crowd went along with him. As he approached the town gate, a dead person was being carried out – the only son of his mother, and she was a widow. And a large crowd from the town was with her. When the Lord saw her, his heart went out to her and he said, 'Don't cry.' Then he went up and touched the coffin, and those carrying it stood still. He said, 'Young man, I say to you, get up!' The dead man sat

---

[2] Bruce Milne, *Know the Truth* (Leicester: IVP, 1982), p. 151.

up and began to talk, and Jesus gave him back to his mother. They were all filled with awe and praised God. 'A great prophet has appeared among us,' they said. 'God has come to help his people.' This news about Jesus spread throughout Judea and the surrounding country.

We also see this claim being made after Jesus healed the man born blind. In the investigation which followed, led by the Jewish religious leaders, they question the man and we read in John 9:17, 'Finally they turned again to the blind man, "What have you to say about him? It was your eyes he opened." The man replied, "He is a prophet."'

Jesus was quite willing to accept the title of prophet as, for example, in the passage we considered earlier, in Mark 6:4: 'Jesus said to them, "Only in his home town, among his relatives and in his own house is a prophet without honour."'

Jesus also described himself as a prophet. For example, in Luke 13:31–33:

> At that time some Pharisees came to Jesus and said to him, 'Leave this place and go somewhere else. Herod wants to kill you.' He replied, 'Go tell that fox, "I will drive out demons and heal people today and tomorrow, and on the third day I will reach my goal." In any case, I must keep going today and tomorrow and the next day – for surely no prophet can die outside Jerusalem!'

But it was not completely adequate to designate Jesus as a prophet. He was more than that. At the transfiguration, described in Mark 9:1–8, when Moses and Elijah appeared with Jesus, the words heard from heaven are very important. God said, 'This is my Son . . . Listen to him!' In other words, Jesus was a prophet but of an entirely different order even from the greatest prophets of the Old Testament. The difference was that he not only spoke on behalf of God but was himself God. This difference between himself and the earlier prophets is clear in the way he spoke. Jesus did not say, 'Thus says the Lord.' Instead he said, 'I say to you.' Jesus is the Word as well as one who proclaims the Word. That is to say, the prophetic Word finds expression not only in his teaching but also in his person, because he is the revelation of God.

Priest

In the Scriptures, Jesus is also described as a priest. The best way to highlight this truth is to ask the question, 'How can sinners come into the presence of a holy God?' The answer given by the writer to the Hebrews is that sinners can come into the presence of a holy God because Christ is the great High Priest who has offered a 'once for all' sacrifice to reconcile sinners to God. We shall consider this in more depth in later chapters.

That has implications for our theology and for our practice. We don't need a priest to pray to God on our behalf and so we have pastors and teachers rather than priests. We don't need to offer sacrifices, so we have the Lord's Supper around a table and not a mass before an altar. Put at its simplest, we now have free and unrestricted access into the presence of God. Jesus has made a new and living way for us to come into the presence of God; all the barriers of the old dispensation have gone (Romans 5:1–2; Ephesians 2:18; 3:12).

Even this is not the end of the story. When the Bible tells us that Jesus is our great High Priest and that he is the only mediator between God and man, it is not only speaking about what he did in the past for us on Calvary, but what he continues to do for us now. Jesus continues a ministry of intercession for us before the throne of God (Romans 8:34; Hebrews 7:25; 1 John 2:1). We shall return to this in a later chapter.

King

The Old Testament prophecies said that Messiah would be a king. For example, in Isaiah 9:6–7, we read this:

> For to us a child is born, to us a son is given, and the government will be on his shoulders. And he will be called Wonderful Counsellor, Mighty God, Everlasting Father, Prince of Peace. Of the increase of his government and peace there will be no end. He will reign on David's throne and over his kingdom, establishing and upholding it with justice and righteousness from that time on and for ever. The zeal of the Lord Almighty will accomplish this.

Also, in Jeremiah 30:8–9: '"In that day," declares the Lord Almighty, "I will break the yoke off their necks and will tear off their bonds; no longer will foreigners enslave them. Instead, they will serve the Lord their God and David their king, whom I will raise up for them."'

We see this also in Ezekiel 37:21–25:

> This is what the Sovereign Lord says: I will take the Israelites out of the nations where they have gone. I will gather them from all around and

bring them back into their own land. I will make them one nation in the land, on the mountains of Israel. There will be one king over all of them and they will never again be two nations or be divided into two kingdoms. They will no longer defile themselves with their idols and vile images or with any of their offences, for I will save them from all their sinful backsliding, and I will cleanse them. They will be my people, and I will be their God. My servant David will be king over them, and they will all have one shepherd. They will follow my laws and be careful to keep my decrees. They will live in the land I gave to my servant Jacob, the land where your fathers lived. They and their children and their children's children will live there for ever, and David my servant will be their prince for ever.

A similar thought is in Zechariah 9:9: 'Rejoice greatly, O Daughter of Zion! Shout, Daughter of Jerusalem! See, your king comes to you, righteous and having salvation, gentle and riding on a donkey, on a colt, the foal of a donkey.'

Jesus was welcomed at birth as a king. As we read in Matthew 2:1–2: 'After Jesus was born in Bethlehem in Judea, during the time of King Herod, Magi from the east came to Jerusalem and asked, "Where is the one who has been born king of the Jews? We saw his star in the east and have come to worship him."' This was also what the angel said to Mary as recorded in Luke 1:30–33:

But the angel said to her, 'Do not be afraid, Mary, you have found favour with God. You will be with child and give birth to a son, and you are to give him the name Jesus. He will be great and will be called the Son of the Most High. The Lord God will give him the throne of his father David, and he will reign over the house of Jacob for ever; his kingdom will never end.'

Jesus did not want his kingship to be misunderstood. In John 6:14–15, when the people intended to make him king by force, Jesus withdrew to a mountain by himself. When he was before Pilate, as described in John 18:36–37, Jesus defended his right to be called 'king' but made it clear that his was not a worldly kingdom. He said:

'My kingdom is not of this world. If it were, my servants would fight to prevent my arrest by the Jews. But now my kingdom is from another place.' 'You are a king, then!' said Pilate. Jesus answered, 'You are right in saying I am a king. In fact, for this reason I was born, and for this I came into the world, to testify to the truth. Everyone on the side of truth listens to me.'

At the same time, the kingdom was central to his preaching and teaching. We are told in Mark 1:14–15 that, after John was put in prison, Jesus went into Galilee proclaiming that the kingdom of God was near. Many of his parables are 'parables of the kingdom'. Most striking is the fact that, during the forty days between his resurrection and ascension, the theme of his preaching was the kingdom of God (Acts 1:3). Even in the later apocalyptic literature, the kingship of Jesus was an important theme. We see it, for example, in Revelation 17:14: 'They will make war against the Lamb, but the Lamb will overcome them because he is Lord of lords and King of kings – and with him will be his called, chosen and faithful followers.'

The Son of God

The second part of Peter's answer to Jesus' question at Caesarea Philippi is more of a surprise. To call Jesus the 'Son of the living God' was to introduce language which was indeed found in the Jewish Scriptures but which was not so common as talk of the Messiah, although there are places in the Old Testament where Israel is identified as the son of God and other places where the king is identified as the son of God. Looking back now with the benefit of the New Testament Scriptures, we can begin to understand something of what this statement means. Perhaps even Peter, at the time, did not understand its full depths and implications.

The key point is that the identity of Jesus is bound up with the identity of the Father, as we shall see in chapter four. Jesus is the Son of God in the sense that he is of one being with the Father. To understand this fully we need to understand the Trinity. God is Father, Son and Spirit. There was never a time when God was not Father, Son and Spirit. The relationship between the three persons of the Trinity is an eternal relationship. At a point in human history, however, the Second Person of the Trinity, the Son of God, took human flesh and became a man, without ceasing to be God. Now this is very hard to understand but it is of critical importance for any understanding of the person of Jesus. In the chapters which follow, we shall see that some theologians have sought to make Jesus into a human being and no more. Others have said that he was a God who only pretended to be a man and did not have a real humanity. In both cases, as we shall see, this constitutes a fundamental attack on the truth of Jesus' being and actually destroys the gospel.

The Revealer of God

If we now turn to John 1:1–18 we can note another element in the biblical understanding of Jesus, namely, that Jesus is the revelation of God. This passage is John's way of introducing us to Jesus. Matthew and Luke both begin their gospels with the story of the birth of Jesus in Bethlehem; Mark jumps to the beginning of Jesus' public ministry and so begins with the story of John the Baptist. Here in John's gospel, however, we are introduced to Jesus in a remarkable way as John speaks about the Word of God who became flesh.

John uses the Greek word *logos* to refer to the Second Person of the Trinity. He says that the *logos* was with God in the beginning and indeed was God. Later in the chapter John speaks of how the *logos* became flesh and identifies the *logos* as Jesus of Nazareth. It is very clear that John is identifying Jesus of Nazareth with the Second Person of the Trinity. Of course, there are other passages which identify Jesus as God. Romans 9:5 speaks of 'Christ, who is God over all'. In Titus 2:13 Jesus is described as 'our great God and Saviour, Jesus Christ'. Then in John 20:28, Thomas said to Jesus, 'My Lord and my God!' John goes on to state that the *logos* was not created, a theme repeated in Philippians 2:5–11 and Colossians 1:15–20. He also identifies the *logos* as the one through whom the world was created. Only with a doctrine of the Trinity can we make sense of these passages.

What we learn from the first two verses of John 1 is that Jesus Christ in his person is the revelation of God. It is the claim of this gospel that God has expressed himself most clearly in Jesus Christ because Jesus is himself the living God. In God's fullest revelation of himself, he does not use a prophet or an apostle; he comes himself, so that what Jesus says is coming from the very mouth of the living God himself. This revelation of God brings light and it brings knowledge. Supremely, however, it brings us into a new relationship with God. Later in the passage, in verses 12–13, John says this: 'Yet to all who received him, to those who believed in his name, he gave the right to become children of God – children born not of natural descent, nor of human decision or a husband's will, but born of God.' This is a staggering proposal! John is saying that, through Jesus, we sinners can become the children of God.

In terms of our understanding of who Jesus is, John 1:18 is critical. This is what it says: 'No-one has ever seen God, but God the One and Only, who is at the Father's side, has made him known.' There are two elements in this text. First, no-one has ever seen God and second, Jesus has made him known. Let's look at each of these in turn:

Question four of the Westminster Shorter Catechism asks, 'What is God?' The answer begins, 'God is a Spirit . . .' That answer is drawn from John 4:24, part of Jesus' discussion with a Samaritan woman. Jesus says to her, 'God is spirit, and his worshippers must worship in spirit and in truth.' God does not have a body, so no-one has seen him. Many people, described in the Bible, have heard him speak or seen something of his glory or seen a 'theophany' (the appearance of God in human form, as to Abraham) but no-one has truly seen God as he is in himself. The question remains: If God is a Spirit and cannot be seen, how do we come to know him? The answer given by John, in the second part of verse 18, is that Jesus has made God known. This God who cannot be seen because he is a Spirit has revealed himself. More particularly, we can say that this God has come among us. Jesus is described in Colossians 1:15 as the 'image of the invisible God'. In that same chapter (1:19), we are told that 'God was pleased to have all his fulness dwell' in Jesus. This means that if we want to know what God is like, we must look at Jesus.

All of this points to the uniqueness of Christ. It means that the only way to obtain real knowledge of God is through Jesus, the only way to meet with God is through Jesus and the only way to be reconciled to God is through Jesus. There can be no talk of God without talking of Jesus. Christianity stands or falls on the identity of Jesus.

Why did he come?

The final question to be asked in this introductory chapter is this: 'Why did Jesus come?' There are various ways in which we might answer this question but the answer given in 1 Timothy 1:15 is the simplest: 'Christ Jesus came into the world to save sinners'. The context of this statement is a passage where Paul gives something of his testimony to the grace of God:

> I thank Christ Jesus our Lord, who has given me strength, that he considered me faithful, appointing me to his service. Even though I was once a blasphemer and a persecutor and a violent man, I was shown

mercy because I acted in ignorance and unbelief. The grace of our Lord was poured out on me abundantly, along with the faith and love that are in Christ Jesus. Here is a trustworthy saying that deserves full acceptance: Christ Jesus came into the world to save sinners – of whom I am the worst (1 Timothy 1:12–15).

Paul saw himself as the 'chief of sinners' but he knew that Christ had come for sinners and that he had been 'saved'. Notice the words 'grace' and 'mercy' in his testimony. Paul understood that his salvation came as a direct result of God's grace and mercy. Not all human beings accept the label 'sinner'. There are those who imagine that they are not sinners. For that reason, it is important to understand this theme which Paul spells out: Christ Jesus came into the world to save sinners, with the implication that those who refuse to accept they are sinners cannot be saved. This is well illustrated by the occasion described in Luke 5:29–32, when Jesus was confronted by the Pharisees about the company he was keeping:

> Then Levi held a great banquet for Jesus at his house, and a large crowd of tax collectors and others were eating with them. But the Pharisees and the teachers of the law who belonged to their sect complained to his disciples, 'Why do you eat and drink with tax collectors and "sinners"?' Jesus answered them, 'It is not the healthy who need a doctor, but the sick. I have not come to call the righteous, but sinners to repentance.'

This is also the theme of Luke 15, where Jesus told the parables of the lost sheep, the lost coin and the lost son. The message of the parables is summed up in verse 10 of that chapter: 'there is rejoicing in the presence of the angels of God over one sinner who repents.'

Since this is why Jesus came, we must recognize that the matters before us in this book are both personal and critical. As we study the person and work of Christ from Scripture and as we compare this teaching with Christian theology as expressed in the councils, creeds and confessions of the church, as well as in the writings of individual Christian writers, let us remember that this cannot be reduced simply to an academic exercise. We are dealing here with issues of life and death.

2

The Divinity of Jesus

Introduction

This chapter is on the divinity (or deity) of Jesus, namely, the claim that Jesus is God. We shall begin by looking at the evidence for this claim and then turn to the historical and theological debate which this claim has occasioned.

What is the evidence for this claim?

At the beginning of his ministry, most people treated Jesus as if he were no more than a wandering rabbi from Nazareth. Many people, including his own family, thought that he was mad when he acted and spoke in a way that seemed to make claims to a special status. Nor was it the case that the doubters gradually became convinced of his claims. Indeed, many of those who followed him initially later deserted him and the crowds who cheered him when he entered Jerusalem were quick to cry 'Crucify him!' a week later. Even his disciples seemed to be uncertain as to his identity, despite having seen so much dramatic evidence of his astonishing power, not least people being healed and raised from the dead. There were, however, points when clarity and faith seemed to shine through, for example, as we have seen, in Peter's great declaration at Caesarea Philippi. These points of insight rarely lasted, however, and the same Peter ran away terrified when Jesus was arrested. It was only after the resurrection that the followers of Jesus truly understood and thereafter consistently maintained his identity as the Son of God.

There is, of course, significant biblical evidence for the deity of Christ. In the Synoptic Gospels of Matthew and Luke we have the infancy narratives, which affirm that Jesus was born miraculously, that his mother was a virgin when she gave birth and that the conception of Jesus came about by the action of God the Holy Spirit. In other words, there was an incarnation (God becoming human) such that the one to whom Mary gave birth was God himself. It is also Matthew who records that one of the names given to Jesus was Immanuel, meaning 'God with us' (Matthew 1:23). Neither Mark's nor John's gospel contains an infancy narrative but the prologue to John's gospel has perhaps the strongest statement of the deity of Jesus. In John 1:1–3 we read, 'In the beginning was the Word, and the Word was with God, and the Word was God. He was with God in the beginning. Through him all things were made; without him nothing was made that has been made.' It is clear from the later verses in the prologue (14–18) that the *logos* referred to in these verses is Jesus of Nazareth. John is thus claiming that Jesus is God and that he was the agent of creation itself.

Some of the most significant biblical references regarding the deity of Christ are found in John's gospel where, as we saw in chapter one, the identity of Jesus was a recurring issue. In controversy with the Jewish leaders, Jesus makes strong claims. For example, in John 8:56–58 he says, '"Your father Abraham rejoiced at the thought of seeing my day; he saw it and was glad." "You are not yet fifty years old," the Jews said to him, "and you have seen Abraham!" "I tell you the truth," Jesus answered, "before Abraham was born, I am!"' The Jews to whom he was speaking knew that this name 'I am' was the name God had used to describe himself when he called Moses to go to Pharaoh (Exodus 3:14). The same claim is made in John 10:30 when Jesus said, 'I and the Father are one.' The Jews understood precisely what Jesus was saying: he was claiming to be God. This is made evident by the fact that, on both occasions, they picked up stones to stone him and, in the latter instance, when challenged by Jesus as to why they were doing this, they replied that they were stoning him, 'because you, a mere man, claim to be God' (John 10:33).

Jesus taught his disciples that he was God. This is demonstrated by one very important encounter, recorded in John 14:8–10, where we find that the disciples themselves wanted proof of Jesus' identity:

> Philip said, 'Lord, show us the Father and that will be enough for us.' Jesus answered: 'Don't you know me, Philip, even after I have been among you such a long time? Anyone who has seen me has seen the Father. How can you say, "Show us the Father"? Don't you believe that I am in the Father, and that the Father is in me? The words I say to you

are not just my own. Rather, it is the Father, living in me, who is doing his work. Believe me when I say that I am in the Father and the Father is in me; or at least believe on the evidence of the miracles themselves.'

For orthodox Christological and Trinitarian thinking, it is imperative to insist that there is no God 'lying behind' Jesus to whom he points but rather that he is himself the revelation of the living God. In other words, God reveals himself in and through himself. Jesus is himself God and so when the disciples looked into the face of Jesus, they were looking into the face of God. Jesus is the very incarnation of the living God.

The other reference in John's gospel which is significant for an understanding of the deity of Christ is John 17:5. In this great prayer of Jesus, often called his 'high priestly prayer', Jesus prays in these words: 'And now, Father, glorify me in your presence with the glory I had with you before the world began.' This surely calls to mind John 1:1–3, which also speaks of his pre-human history in God. If these verses leave some unpersuaded, nothing could be more straightforward than Jesus' words in John 6:38: 'For I have come down from heaven . . .'

There are references in the other gospels which are also important. In Matthew 26:62–64 there is an encounter between Jesus and the high priest in which Jesus is asked a direct question: 'I charge you under oath by the living God: Tell us if you are the Christ, the Son of God.' There is no hesitation in Jesus' answer: 'Yes, it is as you say.' There is a similar encounter with the teachers of the law in Mark 2:5–7, where Jesus heals a paralytic man and forgives his sins. The teachers of the law regarded this as blasphemy because only God can forgive sins. They did not realize that he was God!

It is in the epistles, however, that the clearest statements about Jesus' deity are to be found. This is surely what we would expect. After the momentous events of the resurrection and ascension and after a time of prayer and theological reflection, the earliest Christians were able to express very clearly what the Holy Spirit had given them to understand. We should note particularly that these epistles were written by a range of authors.

The writer to the Hebrews affirms a 'high Christology'. In other words, almost everything he writes is centred on the supremacy and uniqueness of Christ as the final revelation of God. Were we to go through the whole epistle we could see the comparisons he makes between Jesus and the angels, between Jesus and Moses, between

Jesus and the high priest and so on, all to the same effect, namely, the superiority of Jesus because of his deity. Indeed this theme appears in the opening verses of the epistle where we read this:

> In the past God spoke to our forefathers through the prophets at many times and in various ways, but in these last days he has spoken to us by his Son, whom he appointed heir of all things, and through whom he made the universe. The Son is the radiance of God's glory and the exact representation of his being, sustaining all things by his powerful word . . . (Hebrews 1:1–3).

Notice, Jesus Christ is the precise imprint of the nature of God and he upholds the universe. In case there is any doubt, we go on a few verses to Hebrews 1:8, where Jesus is directly addressed as God: 'But about the Son he says, "Your throne, O God, will last for ever and ever, and righteousness will be the sceptre of your kingdom."'

In the introductory greeting to his second epistle, Peter makes a similar affirmation, by describing the recipients of his letter in this way: 'To those who through the righteousness of our God and Saviour Jesus Christ have received a faith as precious as ours' (2 Peter 1:1). Notice these vital words. As far as Peter is concerned, Jesus is 'God and Saviour'. Paul uses the same expression when he writes to Titus, in Titus 2:13, saying that 'we wait for the blessed hope – the glorious appearing of our great God and Saviour, Jesus Christ'. There it is again: Jesus is our 'God and Saviour'. Paul has another striking affirmation of Christ's deity in Romans 9:5, where he speaks of Christ, 'who is God over all . . .'

Paul also expresses a very high Christology in such passages as Ephesians 1:20–23 when he says that God raised Christ:

> from the dead and seated him at his right hand in the heavenly realms, far above all rule and authority, power and dominion, and every title that can be given, not only in the present age but also in the one to come. And God placed all things under his feet and appointed him to be head over everything for the church, which is his body, the fulness of him who fills everything in every way.

This is clearly not the description of a mere man!

Even more striking is Colossians 1:15–20 where Paul affirms that Jesus 'is the image of the invisible God', that he was the agent of creation, that he holds everything in being and that he is in all things pre-eminent. Paul concludes this great peroration by saying, in verse 19, 'For God was pleased to have all his fulness dwell in him'. There can surely be no doubt that Paul was affirming Christ's deity. If there was to be any doubt, it must surely be dispelled by what we find shortly afterwards in Colossians 2:9: 'For in Christ all the fulness of the Deity lives in bodily form'.

The most important passage in Paul's writings concerning the true identity of Jesus is found in Philippians 2:5–11. Using Christ as the example of supreme humility, Paul writes:

> Your attitude should be the same as that of Christ Jesus: Who, being in very nature God, did not consider equality with God something to be grasped, but made himself nothing, taking the very nature of a servant, being made in human likeness. And being found in appearance as a man, he humbled himself and became obedient to death – even death on a cross! Therefore God exalted him to the highest place and gave him the name that is above every name, that at the name of Jesus every knee should bow, in heaven and on earth and under the earth, and every tongue confess that Jesus Christ is Lord, to the glory of God the Father.

This passage also speaks of the pre-existence of Christ in the being of God. Jesus is equal with God in being (ontologically) and yet willingly became a human being. The enormity of this statement can barely be understood with our feeble human minds, yet it remains the core declaration of the Christian faith: Jesus is God.

The teaching of the Bible is quite clear, then, that Jesus is God and that he claimed this for himself. Quite apart from specific texts, however, one key aspect of the evidence for Jesus' divinity is the use of the title 'Lord'.

The word 'Lord' in the Old Testament

In the Old Testament, there are two Hebrew words which came to be translated as 'Lord' in our English Bibles. The first is the word *Adonai*, which means 'master'. This is a general word which is used sometimes to refer to God but is also used to refer to human beings. If you are using a modern English translation of the Bible, then you will know if the word 'Lord' is a translation of *Adonai* if it has a capital 'L' but the other letters are in lower case. The second word translated as 'Lord' is the Hebrew word *YHWH*. This word consists of four Hebrew

letters and no-one is quite sure how it should be pronounced. In the
Authorised Version of the Bible it was rendered as 'Jehovah'. Most
Hebrew scholars now believe that it should be 'Yahweh'. There are
two reasons why we're not sure how to pronounce it: first, vowels
were not part of the original Hebrew text of Scripture; and second,
from about two hundred years before Christ was born, the Jews considered the name of God so sacred that they would not speak the
word. It was written down but never spoken.

When 'Lord' is a translation of *Yahweh* in our English Bibles, it is
rendered in capital letters. This means that in English we can tell
whether the word being translated is *Adonai* or *Yahweh*. This is most
clearly illustrated in Exodus 4:10: 'Moses said to the LORD, "O Lord, I
have never been eloquent . . ."' The first time the word 'LORD' appears
it is in capital letters because the Hebrew word being translated is
Yahweh but then the word 'Lord' appears with only a capital 'L'
because it is a translation of the word *Adonai*.

The word 'Lord' in the New Testament

When the title 'Lord' is used in the New Testament, it is almost
always being used to mean 'master'. This was a common form of
address, particularly to rabbis or important people. It was used in
much the same way that we might use the word 'sir'. Sometimes,
however, when the writers of the New Testament refer to Jesus as
Lord, they are saying more than this: they are testifying to his divinity. In other words, sometimes when they say Jesus is Lord, they are
saying that Jesus is Yahweh. In Paul's great sermon on the Day of
Pentecost, he is commending Jesus to his listeners. In the sermon,
he quotes from Joel 2:28–32 and says, 'everyone who calls on the
name of the Lord will be saved' (Acts 2:21). In the original quotation from Joel, the word used for 'Lord' is *Yahweh* but in Acts the
passage is speaking about Jesus, so the implication is that Jesus *is*
Yahweh.

This interpretation is supported by what we find in Romans
10:1–13. In verses 9–10 of that passage we find these words: 'if you
confess with your mouth, "Jesus is Lord," and believe in your heart
that God raised him from the dead, you will be saved. For it is with
your heart that you believe and are justified, and it is with your
mouth that you confess and are saved.' According to Paul's teaching here, to confess that Jesus is Lord is the way of salvation. Now
is Paul saying that we should confess Jesus as our Master or is he

saying that we should confess Jesus as our God (or both)? The
answer is found in verses 11–13: 'As the Scripture says, "Anyone
who trusts in him will never be put to shame." For there is no difference between Jew and Gentile – the same Lord is Lord of all and
richly blesses all who call on him, for, "Everyone who calls on the
name of the Lord will be saved."' Paul here quotes that passage
from Joel 2 which, as we saw a moment ago, is also quoted in the
Acts of the Apostles chapter 2. Joel is saying that everyone who calls
upon the name of Yahweh will be saved. Paul is saying that everyone who calls on the name of Jesus will be saved. If we understand
that Jesus is God, then there is no contradiction between these statements.

Another important passage is 1 Corinthians 1:1–9, especially the
opening words of greeting: 'To the church of God in Corinth, to those
sanctified in Christ Jesus and called to be holy, together with all those
everywhere who call on the name of our Lord Jesus Christ – their
Lord and ours: Grace and peace to you from God our Father and the
Lord Jesus Christ.' Notice that the believers are addressed as those
who 'call on the name of our Lord Jesus Christ'. This is an expression
meaning worship. To call on the name of Jesus is to worship him.
Since it was deeply rooted in Jewish religious life that only God
could be called upon in worship, it is clear that Jesus is here being
affirmed as God. He is the Lord (Yahweh) and so we must call on
him.

One final passage worth noting is 1 Corinthians 12:3: 'Therefore I
tell you that no-one who is speaking by the Spirit of God says, "Jesus
be cursed," and no-one can say, "Jesus is Lord," except by the Holy
Spirit.' What does this mean? Paul is saying that to affirm Jesus as
Lord is only possible through the work of the Holy Spirit in our lives.
In other words, it is only when we are born again of the Holy Spirit
and indwelt by the Holy Spirit that we can make this affirmation.
This must mean that Paul is using the word 'Lord' here to say that
Jesus is God. After all, if he was simply using the word in its common
sense of 'sir' or 'master' why would it require a work of the Holy
Spirit? As we saw in chapter one, at Caesarea Philippi when Peter
declared that Jesus was the Christ, the Son of the living God, Jesus
immediately said that Peter could only have known this because it
had been revealed to him by God. In the same way, in this statement
in 1 Corinthians 12, Paul is saying that we can only recognize that
Jesus is Lord (meaning God) when it is revealed to us by the Holy
Spirit.

Historical and theological debate

The claim that Jesus is God has been controversial in Christian history. In the earliest days of the Christian church there were those who denied the full deity of Jesus. One significant group was the Ebionites. These were Jewish Christians who believed that Jesus was the son of Mary and Joseph but only became the Son of God at his baptism. In their view, Christ was not divine and they regarded him mainly as a teacher of important religious truths. One of their concerns was the Jewish belief in one God (monotheism) which they believed to be compromised by any teaching that Jesus was God. The strength of Jewish monotheism at that time must not be underestimated here. It was, after all, that which distinguished them from all the other nations and all other religions. The great statement of this is found in Deuteronomy 6:4: 'Hear, O Israel: The LORD our God, the LORD is one.'

The most famous of the Ebionites was Cerinthus. In his view, the Christ who came upon the man Jesus at his baptism, departed again before the crucifixion. Cerinthus and many others were strongly influenced by a philosophy called Gnosticism. This philosophy was based on a Hellenistic (Greek) way of thinking which viewed the soul as a divine 'spark' which, on its journey back to God from our world, had to pass through many spheres. My old professor of church history at Aberdeen University, James McEwan, said their picture resembled an onion with many layers before you reached the core! One of the key beliefs of the Gnostics, which affects our subject here, was that spirit was good and matter was bad. Indeed their whole understanding of salvation was that the soul would escape the body and be absorbed into 'pure spirit'. Since God was pure spirit and could not possibly become a human being, Jesus (who was a human being) must have been a man taken up and used by God and could certainly not have been the incarnation of God.

This view was similar to that held by the 'adoptionists', who argued that Jesus was a good man adopted by God for his purposes. Some of the adoptionists said that the Holy Spirit came down on Jesus at his baptism and left at his crucifixion, while others argued that he was deified after the resurrection. One form of adoptionism, called 'dynamic monarchianism', was expounded by Paul of Samosata, who was condemned by the church as a heretic at Antioch in AD 268. Others claim to see elements of adoptionism in the Antiochene school of theology, including the works of Theodore of Mopsuestia and Nestorius. As we shall see in later chapters, the two great catechetical

schools of the day (which in some ways resembled our modern theological colleges), at Antioch and Alexandria, emphasized different
elements of the truth about Jesus Christ and so often found themselves in conflict.

The greatest controversy in the history of the Christian church in
respect of the deity of Christ took place when Arius, a presbyter from
Alexandria, denied the claim to deity and said that Jesus was simply
the 'firstborn' of God's creation. He gave a high status to Jesus but
denied his deity. This led to a response by Bishop Alexander of
Alexandria and the controversy ultimately led to a council of the
church being called at Nicaea in AD 325. That council rejected Arius'
views and reaffirmed the deity of Christ but the struggle lasted many
years, with the theologian Athanasius bearing the heat of the battle
against the Arians and ultimately triumphing over them. We shall
look in detail at this controversy in chapter four, when we turn our
attention to the important debates at Nicaea, Constantinople and
Chalcedon.

From the end of the fourth century until the nineteenth century this
teaching that Jesus is God was affirmed by virtually all of the churches and went largely unchallenged. In the post-Reformation period,
however, the deity of Christ was challenged by some. At the end of
the sixteenth century a rationalist movement grew up, centred initially on Faustus Socinius. The theology he developed had no place for
a divine Jesus. The modern expression of Socinianism is the Unitarian
Church in its various forms, where the doctrine of the Trinity is rejected and Jesus is regarded as a prophet and not as the incarnation of
God.

The rise of liberal theology in the late eighteenth century brought
many challenges to traditional Christian teaching, not least on the
matter of the deity of Christ. Liberal theology was born out of the
influence of Enlightenment thinking, where autonomous human reason became the final arbiter of truth, instead of God speaking by his
Holy Spirit through the Scriptures. Schleiermacher, Ritschl, Harnack
and Hermann were some of the key figures in the early development
of liberal theology. They promoted ways of thinking and criteria for
decision-making which would ultimately lead to a radical rewriting
of Christian theology, to make it agreeable to human reason.

A later German scholar, Rudolph Bultmann, expressed it like this:

> Man's knowledge and mastery of the world have advanced to such an
> extent through science and technology that it is no longer possible for

anyone seriously to hold the New Testament view of the world – in fact, there is no one who does. What meaning, for instance, can we attach to such phrases in the creed as 'descended into hell' or 'ascended into heaven'? We no longer believe in the three-storied universe which the creeds take for granted. The only honest way of reciting the creeds is to strip the mythological framework from the truth they enshrine – that is, assuming that they contain any truth at all, which is just the question that theology has to ask. No one who is old enough to think for himself supposes that God lives in a local heaven. There is no longer any heaven in the traditional sense of the word. The same applies to hell in the sense of a mythical underworld beneath our feet. And if this is so, the story of Christ's descent into hell and of his Ascension into heaven is done with. We can no longer look for the return of the Son of Man on the clouds of heaven or hope that the faithful will meet him in the air (1 Thess. 4:15ff) . . . It is impossible to use electric light and the wireless and to avail ourselves of modern medical and surgical discoveries, and at the same time to believe in the New Testament world of spirits and miracles. We may think we can manage it in our own lives, but to expect others to do so is to make the Christian faith unintelligible and unacceptable to the modern world.[3]

These discussions were, however, largely confined to scholarly monographs and debates in the Academy. They only exploded into full public view when Bishop John A.T. Robinson brought together and popularized some of the work of Rudolph Bultmann, Paul Tillich and Dietrich Bonhoeffer and published a book entitled *Honest to God*. It is a mark of how radical and provocative this book was seen to be at the time, that Robinson, an Anglican bishop, appeared on the front page of many of the daily newspapers when it was published. It is also striking to note that the book, first published in March 1963, was reprinted three times before that month was finished and then reprinted another five times by the end of September 1963, and numerous times since! This is how Robinson spells out his argument:

But suppose the whole notion of 'a God' who 'visits' the earth in the person of 'his Son' is as mythical as the prince in the fairy story? Suppose there is no realm 'out there' from which the 'Man from heaven' arrives? Suppose the Christmas myth (the invasion of 'this side' by 'the other

[3] Hans-Werner Bartsch, ed., *Kerygma and Myth* (London: SPCK, 2nd edn, 1964), pp. 4–5.

side') – as opposed to the Christmas history (the birth of the man Jesus of Nazareth) – has to go? Are we prepared for that?[4]

He went on to suggest that the Christmas story could survive but only as myth, not as a record of historical events. Since then, others have been even more dismissive of the belief that Jesus is God. In the United Kingdom, this move away from traditional beliefs concerning the deity of Christ culminated in the publication of a book entitled *The Myth of God Incarnate*, edited by John Hick and containing essays by senior academics from Oxford, Cambridge and Birmingham. Here is an extract from the preface:

> It is clear to the writers of this book – as to a great many other Christians today – that Christianity has throughout its history been a continuously growing and changing movement . . . The writers of this book are convinced that another major theological development is called for in this last part of the twentieth century. The need arises from growing knowledge of Christian origins, and involves a recognition that Jesus was (as he is presented in Acts 2:21) 'a man approved by God' for a special role within the divine purpose, and that the later conception of him as God incarnate, the Second Person of the Holy Trinity living a human life, is a mythological or poetic way of expressing his significance for us. This recognition is called for in the interests of truth; but it also has increasingly important practical implications for our relationship to the peoples of the other great world religions.[5]

It might be imagined that these books represent the views of a small insignificant minority of scholars and that their position does not impact on the everyday life of the church but this would be untrue. In 150 years, the almost universally accepted teaching of the great creeds and confessions of the Christian church, namely, that Jesus is God, has been abandoned by many scholars in favour of a 'religionless Christianity' in which there is no belief in the supernatural and, therefore, in which Jesus Christ is not God.

[4] J.A.T. Robinson, *Honest to God* (London: SCM, 1963), pp. 67–8.
[5] John Hick, ed., *The Myth of God Incarnate* (London: SCM, 1977), p. ix.

Conclusion

If we take the passages referring to the divinity of Jesus, together with the birth narratives of Matthew and Luke, and view them through the lens of what we read in John 1, Philippians 2, Colossians 1 and Hebrews 1, then the result is a doctrine of incarnation, whereby the Second Person of the Trinity, the eternal Son of God, takes human flesh and becomes the man Jesus of Nazareth. There is therefore a complete identity between the person of the Son of God and the person of Jesus of Nazareth. There is, in fact, only one person.

Jesus claimed to be God and that claim was vindicated by his actions, in healing the sick, raising the dead and forgiving sins. It was also vindicated by the action of God the Father in accepting his sacrifice on the cross and raising him from the dead. The apostles who wrote the New Testament made it clear that Jesus' claim to be God was fundamental to the Christian gospel. Above all, however, as we enter into a growing understanding of the being and purposes of God it becomes very clear that the theological structure of the universe has, at its heart, a man who is God. Everything centres on him.

3

The Humanity of Jesus

Introduction

In the last chapter we discussed the divinity of Jesus. Now we turn our attention to the humanity of Jesus. In chapter five we shall put all of this together when we ask how precisely the two natures (divine and human) are related in the one person of Jesus. In considering the humanity of Jesus Christ there are several important things we must say: first, his humanity was real; second, his humanity was unfallen; and third, his humanity could suffer.

His humanity was real

The New Testament makes it clear that Jesus was a real human being, like us in every respect except one, namely, that he never sinned. Bruce Milne summed up the biblical teaching very simply and strikingly when he said that Jesus 'was a developing foetus in the womb of Mary and came into the world through a human birth canal at the climax of a normal period of gestation and labour.'[1] Milne goes on to give many different proofs of Jesus' real humanity: he was tempted (Matthew 4:1–2); he could be hungry (Matthew 21:18); he grew up in the normal way (Luke 2:52); he could be tired and fall asleep (John 4:5–6; Matthew 8:23,24); he experienced thirst (John 19:28; Matthew 11:19); he could cry (John 11:35); he had real blood (John 19:34); he could suffer (Mark 14:33–36; Luke 22:63; 23:33). Milne also reminds us that Jesus also went through a whole range of human emotions: joy (Luke 10:21); sorrow (Matthew 26:37); love (John 11:5); compassion (Matthew 9:36); astonishment (Luke 7:9); and anger (Mark 3:5).

---

[1] Bruce Milne, *Know the Truth* (Leicester: IVP, 1982), p. 125.

We can also point out Jesus' growth and development. He increased in knowledge just as we do (Luke 2:52). He also had flesh and bones, as he said to his disciples in a post-resurrection appearance, when they thought he was a ghost (Luke 24:38–39). In that same story, he takes fish and eats it, partly to demonstrate to his disciples that he was a real man and not a ghost or a spirit masquerading as a human being.

Most of the references to the humanity of Jesus, however, come in the context of teaching about the incarnation and the atonement. In other words, it is when the writers of Scripture speak about Jesus' coming from heaven, about his birth and about his 'mission' that they speak of the reality of his humanity. We can cite a number of such passages of Scripture but the following are probably the most significant.

In Romans 8:3 Paul expresses his understanding of the nature of the atonement: 'For what the law was powerless to do in that it was weakened by the sinful nature, God did by sending his own Son in the likeness of sinful man to be a sin offering. And so he condemned sin in sinful man'. The point Paul is making is that all humanity had fallen into sin and, in order for redemption to take place, a sin offering was necessary. Furthermore, that sin offering had to be made by one of the very race which had sinned, namely, by a real human being. The offering being made, God would pass judgement on this representative human being, who would be condemned by God. Thus Paul can say that Jesus came 'in the likeness of sinful man' and that God condemned sin 'in sinful man' (in Christ). There is a whole theology of the atonement lying behind these comments, which we shall explore in the second half of the book. The point to be made here is Paul's teaching that Jesus had to become a real man in order to be eligible to make the sin offering on behalf of human beings and to take the punishment for sin on behalf of human beings.

This interpretation is supported by three other statements made by Paul. First, in Galatians 4:4–5 he writes, 'But when the time had fully come, God sent his Son, born of a woman, born under law, to redeem those under law, that we might receive the full rights of sons.' Notice the two assertions here: Jesus was 'born of a woman' and he was 'born under law'. It could hardly be put more clearly. Jesus was born as others are born and as a result he became a Jewish child and later a Jewish man. As such, he was subject to God's law. The second statement is in Philippians 2:7 where Paul says, '[He] made himself nothing, taking the very nature of a servant, being made in human likeness.' The Second Person of the Trinity, the Son of God, 'emptied

himself' and took a human nature and was thus 'made in human likeness.' This is a great mystery which our minds cannot fully comprehend but whatever other depths we might fathom here, it is certainly
an affirmation of the real humanity of Jesus. The third statement
comes in 1 Timothy 3:16, where Paul says: 'Beyond all question, the
mystery of godliness is great: He appeared in a body, was vindicated
by the Spirit, was seen by angels, was preached among the nations,
was believed on in the world, was taken up in glory.' Notice, he
appeared 'in a body'. He was not a ghost; he was not a fiction of the
imagination; he was a real man in a real body.

His humanity was unfallen

Accepting the reality of Jesus' humanity, however, leaves us with an
important question, namely, what kind of humanity was it? One way
of answering the question is to consider two passages of Scripture
which compare Adam and Christ, namely, Romans 5:12–19 and 1
Corinthians 15:21–22, 45–49. In these passages, there is a parallel which
helps us to understand the nature of Christ's humanity. This parallel is
most consistently developed in what has historically been called
'covenant theology' or 'federal theology'. On this interpretation, it is
argued that the humanity of Christ was like that of Adam before the
fall, namely, unfallen humanity. Taking up the language of these two
Pauline passages, the argument is that Jesus Christ came as the 'second
man' and the 'last Adam' in order to reconcile fallen human beings
with God. When Adam stood before God in Genesis 2, God promised
him that if he ate fruit from the forbidden tree he would die, with the
corresponding implication that if he did not eat from it he would live.

The critical point in federal theology is that when God entered into
a relationship with Adam in this way, it was not just with Adam as a
private individual but with Adam as representative head of the whole
human race, including all of those yet to be born. If the prime minister signs an international treaty he does so in a representative capacity and not as a private individual. Even if he ceases to be prime
minister, the treaty stands. Also, the treaty is binding even on those
citizens not yet born when it was signed. Similarly, Adam was the
representative of the human race and so his decision to obey or disobey God would affect the whole human race.

From this point onwards, Adam was 'on probation' and if he had
remained obedient to God then he and all those whom he represented,

being all humanity, would, at the end of the time of probation, have been confirmed in righteousness, placed beyond the possibility of sin and disobedience and they would have entered into the kind of existence promised for all Christian believers after death.

When Adam sinned by eating from the forbidden tree, as described in Genesis 3, God's judgement fell not only upon Adam but upon all those whom he represented, including us. That is why all human beings are born with what has been called 'original sin'. This means that we have a fallen and corrupt nature which inevitably leads to sin and death. It also means, of course, that death is an enemy (the 'last enemy' says Paul in 1 Corinthians 15:26), an intruder into God's world. This intrusion, however, is only temporary. When we come to the last book of the Bible, we find a picture being drawn of the new Jerusalem, the new heaven and the new earth in which 'he will wipe away every tear from their eyes. There will be no more death or mourning or crying or pain, for the old order of things has passed away' (Revelation 21:4). But how is this to be accomplished? The answer is found in 1 Corinthians 15:21–22, where we read these words: 'For since death came through a man, the resurrection of the dead comes also through a man. For as in Adam all die, so in Christ all will be made alive.' This parallel between Adam and Christ is vital to our understanding of sin and salvation. It is the axis around which the whole Bible revolves.

As Paul explains in those passages from Romans 5 and 1 Corinthians 15, God sent Jesus Christ to take the place of the first Adam and effectively to begin again. By this reading of the Bible, Christ takes the same humanity that Adam had before the fall, namely, unfallen humanity. Like Adam he was without sin and perfectly free to choose to obey God or to disobey God. He did not have original sin or a corrupt nature. The virgin birth guaranteed that he was a real human being but also ensured that he was not 'in Adam'. That is to say, he was not included among those represented by Adam and hence did not inherit a sinful and corrupt nature.

As the 'last Adam', Christ obeyed where Adam had disobeyed and succeeded where Adam had failed. He thus obtained a righteousness before God. In addition to this, as we shall see in the second part of the book, he paid the penalty on the cross for all those who will be in heaven, namely those who, by faith in him, enter into a right relationship with God. When this happens, he takes our sin and gives to us his righteousness. This 'great exchange' means that from then on believers are 'in Christ' and no longer 'in Adam'. This is vital because, as Paul makes clear in 1 Corinthians 15:22, all those who are in Adam will die but all those who are in Christ will be made alive.

This 'federal theology' interpretation has not gone unchallenged. Some have argued that in order to redeem fallen humanity, Christ had to take fallen humanity. This was the view of Professor T.F. Torrance who taught in Edinburgh University and served as moderator of the General Assembly of the Church of Scotland.[2]

Torrance's argument was drawn largely from the Greek fathers of the church, particularly Athanasius and has three main strands. First, when in John 1:14 we read that the Word became 'flesh', Torrance would argue that the Greek word *sarx* here, translated as 'flesh', means not just flesh but sinful flesh. His view was that Christ had to take fallen humanity in order to redeem fallen humanity. He argued, following Gregory of Nazianzus (c. AD 330–90), that 'the unassumed is the unredeemed'. In other words, unless Jesus Christ took our fallen humanity, he had not redeemed us from that fallen humanity. After all, if human beings are in the grip of sin and their natures have become corrupt, how could an unfallen Christ identify with them and save them? Second, Torrance argued that we must appreciate the saving significance of the incarnation. By this argument, when Jesus Christ was incarnated and took fallen humanity, reconciliation had begun to take place in his very person. That is to say, God and fallen humanity were reconciled in the very being of Christ because he was both God and a fallen human being at the same time. Third, Torrance argues that the way in which human beings enter into the saving significance of Christ's being and work is by union with Christ. In other words, as we are united to Christ, we benefit from and share in his reconciled humanity. The way in which Torrance related this to the significance of the cross and resurrection will be considered later.

Torrance's view is common today but when Edward Irving, a Church of Scotland minister, put forward more or less the same position, he was deposed from the ministry of the Church of Scotland in 1833. In one of the tracts he issued during the controversy surrounding his views, he wrote:

> our Lord took the same nature, body and soul, as other men, and under the same disadvantages of every sort, that his flesh was mortal and corruptible, and passive to all our temptations; that his soul was joined to his flesh according to the same laws, and under the same conditions, as

[2] See T.F. Torrance, *Incarnation* (ed. R.T. Walker; Milton Keynes:Paternoster, 2008).

ours is – in one word, that his human will had lying against it, and
upon it, exactly the same oppressions of devil, world, and flesh, which
lay against and upon Adam's will after he had fallen, and which lies
upon every man's will unto this day.

The words 'after he had fallen' are the key to this particular view of
Christ's humanity.

One can feel the strength and challenge of the views of Irving and
Torrance as they genuinely seek to wrestle with the meaning of
Scripture and the nature of the incarnation. Nevertheless, the interpretation of Scripture offered by federal theology remains the more per-
suasive view. It is difficult to read Romans 5 and 1 Corinthians 15, as
well as other passages, without concluding that Christ took exactly the
same pre-fall humanity as Adam. It is also difficult to see in Scripture
Torrance's strong emphasis on the saving significance of the incarnation. The New Testament always seems to place the emphasis on the
cross and the resurrection. This is not to say that the old federal theology is to be preferred in every area of discussion but it certainly seems
to be right about the humanity of Christ.[3]

His humanity could suffer

The reason why Jesus took a human nature was so that he could suffer and die as one of us, in our place. Had he simply come as the
divine Christ, the Second Person of the Trinity, this would have been
impossible. The purpose of his taking human nature, then, was to suffer and die and, had he not taken a human nature, the death he died
would have been ineffective and would not have led to our justification.

The suffering of Jesus did not begin on the cross. Throughout his
life there was suffering. We see it most clearly in the story of
Gethsemane, which took place a short time before the cross. In Mark
14:32–42 we learn that Jesus took his disciples to a place called
Gethsemane and asked them to wait while he prayed. He then took
three of the disciples (Peter, James and John) along with him and went
a little further. Clearly in a state of severe distress, he then asked these
three to wait while he himself went still further, to pray. By so doing

---

[3] The writer is currently working on a volume called *Headship Theology* which seeks
to reconstruct the old federal theology.

he was, in effect, creating a double circle of prayer around him as he went through an agony of soul. Several times during this period of prayer he returned to his disciples and found them asleep. They had not realized the significance of what was about to happen, and Jesus warned them of the danger of weakness: 'The spirit is willing,' he said, 'but the body is weak.'

While Jesus was praying by himself in Gethsemane, he prayed that, if possible, he might be delivered from what was about to happen. He said, '*Abba*, Father, everything is possible for you. Take this cup from me. Yet not what I will, but what you will.' In other words, Jesus was asking God his Father to permit him a way of escape from the suffering and the crucifixion which lay ahead of him. Nevertheless, he was prepared to go the way of the cross if that was what his Father wanted.

These, then, are the facts of Gethsemane. In order to understand the significance of the story we must turn to Hebrews 5:1–10. The key verses in relation to Gethsemane are verses 7–9 where the writer says, 'During the days of Jesus' life on earth, he offered up prayers and petitions with loud cries and tears to the one who could save him from death, and he was heard because of his reverent submission. Although he was a son, he learned obedience from what he suffered and, once made perfect, he became the source of eternal salvation for all who obey him'. Note what is being said here: Jesus cried to God, was heard because of his reverent submission and he learned obedience from what he suffered. It is these concepts of submission and obedience which take us to the heart of the meaning of Gethsemane. Incidentally, when it says that Jesus 'learned' obedience it does not mean that he had previously been disobedient. It means simply that when his willingness to obey God the Father was put to the test, he was not found wanting.

The very word 'Gethsemane' rings a chord in our hearts because it represents the agony which the Lord went through as he faced the cross. He knew what was going to happen and he was afraid because he was facing all the powers of darkness and evil. We might say that the confrontation between God and the devil was to take place in the person of Jesus Christ on the cross at Calvary. If we read the gospel and follow Jesus on his way to Jerusalem and to the cross, we see clearly that it was a spiritual struggle and not simply a physical one.

We must emphasize, however, that the agony of Gethsemane and Jesus' desire to be free from the obligation to go to the cross was not because he was physically afraid but because he was to be the bearer of sin, receiving in his own person the punishment for sin which was rightfully ours. I well remember a sermon on this subject by the Rev. Eric Alexander, then minister of St George's Tron Church of Scotland in Glasgow. Speaking about this story of Jesus in the garden of Gethsemane, he pointed out that many thousands of Christian martyrs have gone to their deaths willingly because they were dying in the service of their Lord and knew that ultimately they had nothing to fear. Is it possible, asked Mr Alexander, that the one who inspired them should be a coward where they were brave, should be reluctant where they were willing and should seek to avoid death when they went to it with heads held high? Mr Alexander underlined the point that the agony of Gethsemane was the agony of bearing the sins of others, the agony of separation from the Father and the agony of bearing in his own person the penalty for sins.

The suffering of Jesus was not only the physical suffering of the scourging, the beating and the cross itself; it was also the suffering of one who stood in the place of human beings and took upon himself all the judgement of God on sin. In one of the 'Suffering Servant' passages in Isaiah, the prophet speaks of a man in these words: 'the LORD has laid on him the iniquity of us all' (Isaiah 53:6). In Christian theology this is taken to be a prophecy about Jesus. As Paul put it, 'He was delivered over to death for our sins' (Romans 4:25); and again, 'God made him who had no sin to be sin for us' (2 Corinthians 5:21).

We shall return to this in the latter part of the book but the climax of this suffering comes on the cross itself. Jesus, who has become sin for us, takes the judgement of God in our place and, in some mysterious fashion that we cannot comprehend, there is a breach within the very being of the Trinity, as the Father punishes the Son instead of punishing us. No wonder that Jesus cries out, 'My God, my God, why have you forsaken me?' (Matthew 27:46).

The most significant aspect of Gethsemane was the obedience which Jesus rendered to the Father. Or, to put it another way, it was the victory over self which Jesus won at Gethsemane. He was willing to endure the cross because it was the will of his Father. He was prepared to be the Lamb which was sacrificed for sin and he was prepared to shed his blood in order that we might be saved. Jesus made it clear that he was not compelled to do this but did so freely out of the love which flows from the Father. As Jesus says in John 10:17–18, 'The reason my Father loves me is that I lay down my life – only to take it up again. No-one takes it from me, but I lay it down of my own accord. I have authority to lay it down and authority to take it up again. This command I received from my Father.'

So, then, at Gethsemane Jesus asked to be delivered, but he was prepared to go the way of the cross if that was what his Father required: 'not my will, but yours be done' (Luke 22:42). In this sense, Gethsemane was a foretaste of the cross. On the cross, Jesus rendered obedience to God the Father by allowing himself to be crucified. The theologians call this the 'passive obedience' of Christ, as we shall see in more detail later. The decision to render that obedience was made at Gethsemane. Gethsemane was the last point on the way to the cross at which Jesus could have turned back. It was at Gethsemane that he struggled against the world, the flesh and the devil before taking that long, lonely journey to Calvary. It was at Gethsemane that he determined to go the way of the cross. There can be no doubt about the reality of his suffering and pain and therefore there can be no doubt about his true humanity.

Historical and theological debate

The humanity of Jesus has never been as controversial as the claim that he is divine and there is virtually no-one today who seriously doubts the real humanity of Jesus. In our modern world it is the deity of Christ which is attacked and not his humanity. Nevertheless, there have been those in the past who denied it. As noted in the last chapter, the gospel came into a society where Hellenistic thought was dominant. When the first Christians taught that God had become flesh, in the person of Jesus Christ, those influenced by such thinking simply could not accept this teaching.

Some of those influenced by Hellenistic thinking wanted to be Christians and so they tried to adjust the message about Jesus to make it fit with their ideas. They said that Jesus was not a real man but only 'seemed' to be a man. These people were called 'docetists' (from the Greek, meaning 'to seem'). They believed that Jesus was a spirit who only pretended to be a man. This was one of the earliest Christian heresies and it was deeply damaging to the gospel. It made its appearance before the last few books of the New Testament were written, so that the apostle John could address the issue in 1 John 4:2–3: 'This is how you can recognise the Spirit of God: Every spirit that acknowledges that Jesus Christ has come in the flesh is from God, but every spirit that does not acknowledge Jesus is not from God. This is the spirit of the antichrist, which you have heard is coming and even now is already in the world.'

Some others who denied the real humanity of Jesus were called 'monarchians'. They received this name because they wanted to emphasize the sole 'monarchy' or rule of the Father. This group flourished around AD 200. There were two types of monarchians: the 'dynamic monarchians' and the 'modalistic monarchians'. The first type, dynamic monarchians, taught a kind of adoptionism, of which the most notable exponent was Paul of Samosata, the Bishop of Antioch, as we saw in the last chapter. They held views similar to those of the Ebionites and adoptionists.

Whereas the dynamic monarchians denied the deity of Christ, the modalistic monarchians (or 'modalists') also denied his real humanity. They believed that Father, Son and Spirit were merely three 'modes' or 'masks' worn by God but argued that there is nothing in the being of God that corresponds to this threefold division. This belief was also called 'patripassianism' because its denial of the Trinity was taken to mean that God the Father was crucified! At the beginning of the third century this heresy was called 'Sabellianism', named after one of its leading exponents, Sabellius. Another significant modalist was Praxeas. The early theologians Tertullian and Hippolytus were the main opponents of monarchianism, and most of what we know about the movement comes from their writings.

Conclusion

These heretical views were largely disposed of by the church by the end of the third century but finally declared to be unorthodox at the great councils of Nicaea and Chalcedon. The biblical and theological evidence for the humanity of Jesus is overwhelming and, as we shall see when we come to discuss the atonement, is vital for our salvation.

4

The Second Person of the Trinity

Introduction

The early church, in seeking to interpret Scripture, was faced with the two realities expressed in the previous two chapters, namely, that Jesus is both God and man. In exploring this, it became clear that the only way in which a full and proper understanding of Jesus could be obtained was to begin with the being of God. In other words, Jesus cannot be understood unless we begin with the Trinitarian being of God and work from there.

In this chapter we are going to open up this Trinitarian starting point. After a general introduction to the doctrine of the Trinity, we shall do three things. First, we shall consider the relationship between Jesus and the Father, dealing with the claim that Jesus is the eternal Son of God. Second, we shall consider the relationship between Jesus and the Holy Spirit, dealing with Jesus' conception, baptism and ministry. Then, third, we shall turn to the historical and theological debates which led to the Nicene Creed.

The Trinity

In any doctrine of God, we must begin with the first few words of the Bible: 'In the beginning God created the heavens and the earth.' This means that we must begin our doctrine of God by insisting upon what has been called the 'Creator-creature distinction'. In other words, we begin with the recognition that God is the Creator and is not to be identified with creation. This stands in opposition to pantheism, the view that God is everything and everything is God, an old view which is enjoying a resurgence in several environmental 'green' philosophies and in some new age and neo-pagan spirituality. It also stands in opposition to all forms of theology which would seek to bring God down and to deny his transcendence. The Christian view has always been that God stands over against creation, which he made 'out of nothing' (*ex nihilo*).

The second thing we must say as we build our doctrine of God is that God is not 'knowable' except by revelation. Even then we can never fully 'know' God as he is in himself but only what he chooses to reveal of himself. The only one who knows God completely and exhaustively is God himself. For that reason, revelation is fundamental to Christian theology. If this God who knows himself exhaustively had chosen not to reveal himself, we would have known nothing of him, but if he does choose to reveal himself then what we receive from him is real knowledge because he knows exhaustively. This last point probably requires some elucidation and an illustration might help. A scientist may be in possession of a certain number of facts. It may be, however, that tomorrow the scientist will discover something which either calls into question the facts he thought he possessed, or casts those facts into an entirely new hypothesis. By this means science is changing all the time. No scientist today believes precisely what Copernicus, Galileo or Newton believed. Even Einstein has been overtaken in some aspects of his thinking. For this reason, no scientist can ever claim that he has the final truth. To know anything for certain, you have to know everything! For human beings this is, of course, impossible. Christians affirm, however, that God knows everything. Indeed, when scientists make discoveries they are simply 'thinking God's thoughts after him'. Since God knows everything, what he does reveal to us is absolutely true because there is no fact, no knowledge, no information of which God is unaware.

The third point to be made is that God is not an 'it' or a 'thing'; God is personal. This does not imply that God is like a human being, only on a grand scale. It means rather that God is a subject with whom we as subjects can have a relationship. It means that we can speak of knowing God and being related to God in much the same kind of language that we would use to describe our human relationships. Above all, since God is personal, we can speak of God. That is to say, there can be theology (God talk) as opposed to simply talking sociologically about religion, religious people and religious activities. It is a matter of great regret that some theologians have lost confidence in the ability to speak of God – indeed some no longer believe in a 'god' in the biblical sense. One important implication of the fact that God is personal is that he can never be viewed as an object to be studied and analyzed. Nor can he be reduced to a 'Prime Mover' or a 'First Cause'. Revelation means not only that we obtain knowledge of God but also that we experience the self-disclosure of God. In other words, God is not some being waiting to be discovered by human beings; rather he is a personal God who reveals himself and who encounters us.

With these preliminary points, we can now focus on the doctrine of the Trinity. We must begin by saying that this is not an easy subject and we must come to it in the right frame of mind. It is here, perhaps more than anywhere in theology, that we see the relationship between faith and inquiry. Or, as others have put it, the only true theology is church theology. It is not possible to approach the mystery of the Trinity unless we come as those who believe. This is how A.A. Hodge expressed it at the beginning of his lecture on the Trinity:

> We shall now discuss the revelation which God has made of himself in his inspired Word as three Persons. This we must do with bowed heads and reverent hearts, for the ground on which we stand is holy. The subject is transcendently sacred: it is the infinitely righteous and majestic God. It is immeasurably important as the foundation of all knowledge and faith . . . We can know only just as much of this subject of the Trinity as is definitely set forth in the Bible, and no more. Our office here is that, simply, of humble disciples – to observe and interpret the self-exhibition of the Triune God in Scripture.[1]

The Bible contains a number of references which help us to reach a doctrine of the Trinity but the doctrine is not spelled out in Scripture. As we saw in an earlier chapter, one of the key references in any doctrine of God is Deuteronomy 6:4: 'Hear, O Israel: The LORD our God, the LORD is one.' This verse, very important to the Jews, speaks of the unity of God. There are not three gods, but only one. There are, however, other verses where there appears to be a plurality in the being of God. For example, in Genesis 1:26, we read this: 'Then God said, "Let us make man in our image, in our likeness, and let them rule over the fish of the sea and the birds of the air, over the livestock, over all the earth, and over all the creatures that move along the ground."' Then again, in Genesis 3:22: 'And the LORD God said, "The man has now become like one of us, knowing good and evil. He must not be allowed to reach out his hand and take also from the tree of life and

---

[1] A.A. Hodge, *Evangelical Theology: Lectures on Doctrine* (Edinburgh: Banner of Truth, 1976), p. 97.

eat, and live for ever."' Similarly, Genesis 11:7: 'Come, let us go down and confuse their language so they will not understand each other.' Is this a plurality of being or simply a plurality of grammar (because the word used for 'God', *elohim*, is a plural form)?

Then there are those verses where the Father, Son and Holy Spirit are spoken of together in a 'benediction' format, for example Matthew 28:19: 'Therefore go and make disciples of all nations, baptising them in the name of the Father and of the Son and of the Holy Spirit'. Similarly, 2 Corinthians 13:14: 'May the grace of the Lord Jesus Christ, and the love of God, and the fellowship of the Holy Spirit be with you all.'

As well as the verses which show that the first Christians taught that Jesus is God, which we have already considered in chapter two, there are also verses which teach that the Holy Spirit is God. For example, Mark 3:29: 'But whoever blasphemes against the Holy Spirit will never be forgiven; he is guilty of an eternal sin.' Similarly, John 15:26: 'When the Counsellor comes, whom I will send to you from the Father, the Spirit of truth who goes out from the Father, he will testify about me.' Or what about 1 Corinthians 6:19–20: 'Do you not know that your body is a temple of the Holy Spirit, who is in you, whom you have received from God? You are not your own; you were bought at a price. Therefore honour God with your body.' Finally, 2 Corinthians 3:17–18: 'Now the Lord is the Spirit, and where the Spirit of the Lord is, there is freedom. And we, who with unveiled faces all reflect the Lord's glory, are being transformed into his likeness with ever-increasing glory, which comes from the Lord, who is the Spirit.' It is also very clear from these references that the Holy Spirit is personal, not simply a power or force. The Scripture references above tell us that 'he will' do various things. The Holy Spirit is one who acts, just as the Father acts and the Son acts. He is fully personal and fully God. The church has a bad history of neglect in relation to the person of the Holy Spirit and it was perhaps only in the twentieth century that this was remedied to some extent.

The doctrine of the Trinity has been summed up in the expression: one *substance*, three *persons*. It was Tertullian who originally coined these words (or rather their Latin equivalents), as well as the word 'Trinity' itself. The word 'person' is used to describe Father, Son and Holy Spirit when each is being considered individually. The word 'substance' is used to emphasize their commonality and unity.

Historically, the doctrine of the Trinity was quite late in being finally established. Although Tertullian had, at the very beginning of the

third century, created the vocabulary and outlined the doctrine, it was
not at that stage universally accepted. It was only after the debates
over the person of Christ in the fourth and fifth centuries had concluded with the agreement that he was of one being with the Father,
that the question was then asked: Are there then two Gods? Clearly
the answer was 'no', and so it was necessary to try and understand in
what way Jesus Christ was God. Later, Basil of Caesarea and the
Cappadocians argued strongly for the divinity of the Holy Spirit and
that led to the completion of the doctrine.

This was not universally accepted, of course, as demonstrated by
various heresies which have arisen from time to time. Four of these
stand out as being the most persistent. First, subordinationism, which
refers to the view of those who in any way undermine the full deity
of the Son or the Holy Spirit, or who suggest that the Father is truly
God whereas the Son and the Spirit are only God (if at all) in a somewhat lesser sense. Second, modalism, which refers to the view that the
one God simply appears to us in different forms (or modes). This
gives the picture of one God who wears different masks at different
times and argues that if somehow we were able to 'examine' God, we
would not see anything corresponding to Trinity. Third, tritheism, the
view that there are three beings, each of whom is divine. In other
words, tritheism argues that there are three Gods. Fourth, unitarian-
ism, the view that there is only one God and that Jesus Christ and the
Spirit are not God. On this view, Jesus would be a man used by God
and the Holy Spirit would be regarded as a force or a power from God
but not a distinct person within the godhead.

The doctrine of the Trinity is an extremely difficult doctrine but it
is fundamental to any understanding of Christianity and it is where
we begin. It is not a theological puzzle or conundrum but is the very
heart and centre of all meaning and significance. Even in terms of our
salvation it is vital. The Father loves us so much that he sends his Son.
The Son dies for our sins. The Holy Spirit then applies what Christ
has done to our lives.

Jesus and the Father

As we noted in chapter one, it is vital that we understand what we
mean when we say that Jesus is the Son of God. In the account of the
meeting between Mary and the angel Gabriel, we read these words
from Luke 1:35: 'The Holy Spirit will come upon you, and the power

of the Most High will overshadow you. So the holy one to be born will be called the Son of God.' When Mark came to write his gospel he began with these words: 'The beginning of the gospel about Jesus Christ, the Son of God.' Near the end of his gospel, in John 20:31, the apostle John gives his reason for writing: 'But these are written that you may believe that Jesus is the Christ, the Son of God, and that by believing you may have life in his name.'

Often this title was used against Jesus. In Matthew 4:3–6 we read this:

> The tempter came to him and said, 'If you are the Son of God, tell these stones to become bread.' Jesus answered, 'It is written: "Man does not live on bread alone, but on every word that comes from the mouth of God."' Then the devil took him to the holy city and had him stand on the highest point of the temple. 'If you are the Son of God,' he said, 'throw yourself down. For it is written: "He will command his angels concerning you, and they will lift you up in their hands, so that you will not strike your foot against a stone."'

Similarly, in Matthew 27:39–43, when Jesus was on the cross, we read this:

> Those who passed by hurled insults at him, shaking their heads and saying, 'You who are going to destroy the temple and build it in three days, save yourself! Come down from the cross, if you are the Son of God!' In the same way the chief priests, the teachers of the law and the elders mocked him. 'He saved others,' they said, 'but he can't save himself! He's the King of Israel! Let him come down now from the cross, and we will believe in him. He trusts in God. Let God rescue him now if he wants him, for he said, "I am the Son of God."'

Others, however, used the title as a mark of respect and as a statement of faith. In Matthew 27:54 the centurion responsible for guarding Jesus as he was dying on the cross says, 'Surely he was the Son of God!'

Jesus was happy to accept this title. In Luke 22:67–70 he was challenged by the Sanhedrin:

> 'If you are the Christ,' they said, 'tell us.' Jesus answered, 'If I tell you, you will not believe me, and if I asked you, you would not answer. But from now on, the Son of Man will be seated at the right hand of the

mighty God.' They all asked, 'Are you then the Son of God?' He replied, 'You are right in saying I am.'

This conviction that Jesus was the Son of God also formed an important theme in the preaching of the early church. In Acts 9:19–20 we're told that after Saul was converted on the road to Damascus, he 'spent several days with the disciples in Damascus. At once he began to preach in the synagogues that Jesus is the Son of God.' Having only just become a Christian, this was his theme: 'Jesus is the Son of God.' It is also used in his letters (see 1 Thessalonians 1:9–10 and Romans 1:3–4). In 1 John 4:15 the apostle John goes so far as to make the acknowledgement that Jesus is the Son of God, the evidence of true salvation: 'If anyone acknowledges that Jesus is the Son of God, God lives in him and he in God.' Similarly, in 1 John 5:5 he writes, 'Who is it that overcomes the world? Only he who believes that Jesus is the Son of God.'

All of these Scriptures, taken together, should leave us in no doubt that, as far as Jesus and the apostles were concerned, he is the Son of God. We must go on to make the even more important point that this sonship is eternal. This is a more complicated issue and we might express it in the form of a question: 'Did Jesus become the Son of God when he was born on this earth, or has the Son of God always existed?' This question takes us deep into the heart of the doctrine of the Trinity.

The first theologian to tackle this question was Origen. Origen was one of the Greek fathers of the church. Born and brought up in a Christian family in Egypt, he went to study at the great catechetical school of Alexandria, where Clement was his teacher. Origen later went on to become head of the school in Alexandria and his teaching drew many to hear him. He was also an accomplished writer. Not much of his writing survives and so most of what we know of him comes from what others have written, most notably the history written by Eusebius.

Origen approached the problem in this way. He said that God has always been three persons: Father, Son and Holy Spirit. This naturally raised the question of the relationship between the Father and the Son. On the one hand, Origen wanted to give priority to the Father, so he said that the Son was 'generated' by the Father. On the other hand, he did not want to suggest that the Son had a beginning, so he spoke of an 'eternal' generation, a generation which had no beginning. Now this language is very complex but Origen was pointing to a very important biblical truth, namely, that God is eternal and so all three persons in the godhead must be eternal. It was in the fourth century that Origen's view was challenged, when Arius argued that Jesus was not the eternal Son of God but was a created being. The church spent a long time resolving this as we shall see later, but ultimately it declared Arius to be a heretic and sided with Origen. The Second Person of the Trinity, the Son of God, at a certain point in space and time, took to himself a human nature and was incarnated as the man Jesus of Nazareth. Hence we can say that Jesus is the eternal Son of God.

Jesus and the Holy Spirit

When we come to consider the relationship between Jesus and the Holy Spirit we find four areas of particular interest, namely, the Holy Spirit in the conception of Jesus, the Holy Spirit in the baptism of Jesus, the Holy Spirit in the earthly ministry of Jesus and the Holy Spirit in the ongoing ministry of Jesus.

The Holy Spirit in the conception of Jesus

Have you ever wondered why the Second Person of the Trinity needed the Third Person of the Trinity, in order to become flesh? Or, to put the question another way, why was Jesus 'conceived by the Holy Spirit'? Could not the Second Person of the Trinity have become flesh on his own, without the work of the Third Person?

There is a sense in which the human nature of Jesus was given by the Father, or at least he determined what would happen, as we see in Hebrews 10:5, where Jesus says to the Father, 'a body you prepared for me'. Nevertheless, it was by the Spirit that this body came into existence. What we must remember is that the works of the Trinity – Father, Son and Holy Spirit – are not divided. There is a unity of being and purpose in all that they do. The Holy Spirit acts as the agent of the Trinity in carrying out the will of God. In the matter of the conception of Jesus, it was the Spirit who acted. That is why he can be called 'the Spirit of [the] Son' (Galatians 4:6).

The Holy Spirit formed the body of Christ in the womb of Mary. He was the one who created that human nature, as we saw above in Matthew 1:20: 'what is conceived in her is from the Holy Spirit.' The Holy Spirit having created the human flesh in the womb of Mary, the

Second Person of the Trinity, the Son of God, immediately assumed that human nature into union with his divine nature, as we read in Hebrews 2:14–15: 'Since the children have flesh and blood, he too shared in their humanity . . .' We are used to this doctrine from the words of the Apostles' Creed: 'He was conceived by the Holy Spirit, born of the Virgin Mary.'

The theological significance of the virgin birth is that it guaranteed the sinlessness of Jesus. As we saw in Romans 5 and 1 Corinthians 15, where Paul compares Adam and Christ, all human beings are born as sinners because of the sin of the first man Adam. Jesus Christ came as the second man, the last Adam, and he began a new humanity, such that we are either 'in Adam' or 'in Christ'. Those who are 'in Adam' will die and face an eternity in hell; those who are 'in Christ' have the promise of heaven and eternal life. This, of course, is where the theological issue comes in: if Christ had been born in the normal human way, as the child of Mary, why was he not born as a sinner? The answer is that the virgin birth and the work of the Holy Spirit guaranteed that Jesus was born without sin. In order to be the Saviour of the world he had to be a human being but in order to be the Saviour of the world he had to be without sin. The virgin birth provides the solution to this problem. It enables us to insist, on the one hand, that Christ is descended from Adam (real humanity) but also to insist, on the other hand, that Christ was not among those who were born as sinners because of Adam's sin. The doctrine of the virgin birth enables us to hold both of these propositions without contradiction. The Son of God took to himself our humanity but nothing that was sinful.

The Holy Spirit in the baptism of Jesus

The next key event in the relation between Jesus and the Holy Spirit is the baptism of Jesus. The Scriptures tell us that at his baptism by John in the Jordan, Jesus received the Holy Spirit. As we read in Matthew 3:16–17, 'As soon as Jesus was baptised, he went up out of the water. At that moment heaven was opened, and he saw the Spirit of God descending like a dove and lighting on him. And a voice from heaven said, "This is my Son, whom I love; with him I am well pleased."' In a sermon in Acts 10:37–38, Peter reminds us of that event: 'You know what has happened throughout Judea, beginning in Galilee after the baptism that John preached – how God anointed Jesus of Nazareth with the Holy Spirit and power, and how he went around doing good and healing all who were under the power of the devil, because God was with him.'

The Holy Spirit in the ministry of Jesus

If we now ask why it was that Jesus needed the Holy Spirit, the answer must be that it was to enable his ministry. There is one significant passage in Scripture, Luke 4:1–2, where we see how much the ministry of Jesus was guided and empowered by the Holy Spirit: 'Jesus, full of the Holy Spirit, returned from the Jordan and was led by the Spirit in the desert, where for forty days he was tempted by the devil. He ate nothing during those days, and at the end of them he was hungry.' After the temptations, we are told that 'Jesus returned to Galilee in the power of the Spirit' (Luke 4:14). During the life of Jesus, right up to the cross, a great spiritual battle was taking place. In this major encounter with Satan, the indwelling Holy Spirit empowered and enabled Jesus for the battle.

We should also remember the story of what happened when Jesus returned to his home town of Nazareth and was asked to read the Scripture on the Sabbath in the synagogue. He read Isaiah 61:1–2 and then said that the passage referred to him, thus speaking of his ministry in terms of the work of the Holy Spirit. The passage is quoted in Luke 4:16–21:

> He went to Nazareth, where he had been brought up, and on the Sabbath day he went into the synagogue, as was his custom. And he stood up to read. The scroll of the prophet Isaiah was handed to him. Unrolling it, he found the place where it is written: 'The Spirit of the Lord is on me, because he has anointed me to preach good news to the poor. He has sent me to proclaim freedom for the prisoners and recovery of sight for the blind, to release the oppressed, to proclaim the year of the Lord's favour.' Then he rolled up the scroll, gave it back to the attendant and sat down. The eyes of everyone in the synagogue were fastened on him, and he began by saying to them, 'Today this scripture is fulfilled in your hearing.'

It is because Christ had been endowed with the Holy Spirit that he was able to do great things. First, he was able to speak God's Word because 'God gives the Spirit without limit' (John 3:34). Second, he was able to do miracles because of the Holy Spirit (Matthew 12:28). Third, by the Holy Spirit he was able to offer himself up on the cross

(Hebrews 9:14). Fourth, it was by the Spirit that he was raised from the dead and declared to be the Son of God (Romans 1:1–4). In other words, every aspect of the life and ministry of Jesus was empowered and enabled by the Holy Spirit.

The Holy Spirit in the ongoing ministry of Jesus

We have seen that Jesus was conceived by the Holy Spirit, received the Holy Spirit at his baptism and was empowered by the Holy Spirit throughout his ministry. Now we must make the point that the one who received the Holy Spirit also gives the Holy Spirit.

Jesus promised his disciples, in John 14:15–17, that he would send the Holy Spirit: 'If you love me, you will obey what I command. And I will ask the Father, and he will give you another Counsellor to be with you for ever – the Spirit of truth. The world cannot accept him, because it neither sees him nor knows him. But you know him, for he lives with you and will be in you.' Later in the same passage, in verse 26, he tells them something of the purpose of the coming of the Holy Spirit: 'the Counsellor, the Holy Spirit, whom the Father will send in my name, will teach you all things and will remind you of everything I have said to you.' In John 16:7 Jesus even said to the disciples, 'But I tell you the truth: It is for your good that I am going away. Unless I go away, the Counsellor will not come to you; but if I go, I will send him to you.' He then spelled out, in verses 13–15, what the Holy Spirit would do when he came:

> he will guide you into all truth. He will not speak on his own; he will speak only what he hears, and he will tell you what is yet to come. He will bring glory to me by taking from what is mine and making it known to you. All that belongs to the Father is mine. That is why I said the Spirit will take from what is mine and make it known to you.

As we can see, Jesus received the Holy Spirit and then he gave the Holy Spirit. This, of course, is precisely what was prophesied by John the Baptist in Luke 3:16: 'I baptise you with water. But one more powerful than I will come, the thongs of whose sandals I am not worthy to untie. He will baptise you with the Holy Spirit and with fire.' In John 1:32–33 the words of the Baptist are spelled out in more detail: 'I saw the Spirit come down from heaven as a dove and remain on him. I would not have known him, except that the one who sent me to baptise with water told me, "The man on whom you see the Spirit come down and remain is he who will baptise with the Holy Spirit."'

The final point to be made regarding the relation between Jesus and the Holy Spirit is that Jesus sanctified himself, in order that we might later be sanctified. This is what Jesus said in John 17:19: 'For them I sanctify myself, that they too may be truly sanctified.' The Christian life is a life in which the Holy Spirit acts as the agent for the out-working of the grace of God in the lives of human beings. To this end, he unites us to Jesus Christ, regenerates us, sanctifies us and empowers us for service. In other words, he brings us into the very life of God through our union with Christ. This is what makes the life of the Christian more than a legalistic obedience to law, a keeping of ourselves right with God. Rather, it is about the grace of God made known to us in our experience of transformation and sanctification by the Spirit into a relationship with Jesus Christ, which energizes us and enables us to live for God.

Jesus was conceived by the Holy Spirit, filled with the Holy Spirit at his baptism, empowered by the Holy Spirit throughout his ministry, and offered up himself as a sacrifice to the Father by the Holy Spirit. Having done so, he now sends the Holy Spirit to his people, so that we may be regenerated, sanctified, empowered and, above all, taken up into relationship with God through our participation in Jesus Christ.

Historical and theological debate

The most significant debate in the history of Christology was occasioned by a man called Arius, who was a presbyter of Alexandria.[2] Arius held to a strong monotheistic position and did not believe that Jesus was God. Rather, he believed Jesus to be the first and greatest of all created beings. He was opposed by Alexander, Bishop of Alexandria, who insisted that Jesus was truly divine. Alexander did not deny that Jesus was 'generated' by the Father but insisted that this was an eternal generation.

After much debate, Arius and his followers were excommunicated. By this time, however, Arius had sought and found help and support from outside Egypt and the matter had become more than a local case

---

[2] The most significant treatment of Arius is by the current Archbishop of Canterbury. See Rowan Williams, *Arius: Heresy and Tradition* (London: SCM, 2nd edn, 2001).

of church discipline. In particular, he enlisted the help of a number of bishops who shared his views.

The theologian Athanasius provided the main theological opposition to the views of Arius. Although he was only a young man when the controversy broke out, he had been noticed and promoted by Bishop Alexander of Alexandria and indeed accompanied the bishop to the Council of Nicaea, as his secretary. Although he only went to Nicaea in support of his bishop, even then, and certainly for the next forty years, his was the major theological voice of orthodoxy and he was the principal opponent of Arian and semi-Arian views.

The Council of Nicaea

The Arian controversy was deeply divisive and when Emperor Constantine came to rule over the whole Roman Empire in AD 324, he brought with him a strong desire for a united Christianity in a united empire, and so he called the Council of Nicaea in AD 325 to settle the matter of the relation between the Son and the Father.

Alexander and Athanasius insisted that the way to describe the relationship between the Father and the Son within the godhead was to use the term *homoousios*, which means 'of the same essence (or substance)'. Arius rejected both the term and the idea which lay behind it, arguing that Jesus was a creature and was not of the same essence as the Father. The battle, however, was not just between Arius and his supporters on the one side and Alexander, Athanasius and their supporters on the other side. There was another group in-between, a moderate party, who wanted a compromise. This group (whose members were often called the 'semi-Arians') was led by the great church historian Eusebius, who was a much better historian than he was a theologian. This middle group wanted to substitute the word *homoiousios* for the word *homoousios*. This compromise word meant 'of similar essence'. This dispute over two Greek words underlines the complexity of the matter. Here was a major battle concerning the doctrine of the Trinity and the doctrine of the deity of Christ, yet it rested on one Greek letter! The difference made by this one Greek letter was, of course, colossal. These three groups met at Nicaea to settle the matter once and for all.

The council (after the emperor intervened) concluded that what Alexander and Athanasius said was orthodox; its members rejected the Arian and the semi-Arian positions. The word *homoousios* was affirmed to be correct as a statement of Jesus' relationship to the Father. This meant that the church was stating unambiguously that Jesus Christ was a divine person and was of one essence with the Father.

The aftermath

The matter didn't end there, however, and the arguments raged on. Many within the church were dissatisfied because it was the emperor who had settled the matter, whereas they believed that only the church had the right to determine its doctrine. Hence, for a long time there were Arians and semi-Arians in the church, despite the decisions of Nicaea. Athanasius battled against them but very often was left in a small minority among the bishops and even occasionally entirely alone. It is paradoxical that most Christians were more orthodox than most of their bishops. The various emperors tended to side with the majority view of the bishops and so five times Athanasius was removed from his position and forced into exile.

For a considerable period, the church in the West took the side of Athanasius, whereas the church in the East became more or less completely semi-Arian. Various councils were held to settle the matter but without success. At one point, the emperor Constantius by various means brought the Western bishops into line with the East and so almost the whole of Christendom was opposed to Athanasius and the Nicene party. Eventually, however, this was turned round. This happened partly because the Arian party became more and more divided and because a more extreme group within it came to the fore. Several church fathers were involved in the return to orthodoxy, including Basil, Gregory of Nyssa and Gregory of Nazianzus (called the 'Cappadocian fathers').[3]

The Nicene Creed

The conclusions of this Council of Nicaea were summarized in the first form of the Nicene Creed:

---

[3] For a detailed analysis of the doctrinal controversies of the early church period, see J.N.D. Kelly, *Early Christian Creeds* (London: A&C Black, 1972) and also his *Early Christian Doctrines* (London: A&C Black, 5th edn, 1977).

I believe in one God, the Father Almighty, Maker of heaven and earth, and of all things visible and invisible. And in one Lord Jesus Christ, the only-begotten Son of God, begotten of the Father before all worlds; God of God, Light of Light, very God of very God; begotten, not made, being of one substance with the Father, by whom all things were made.

The Arians had imperial support from AD 353–78 but thereafter declined. The Council of Constantinople met in AD 381 and affirmed Nicene orthodoxy. At this council, several paragraphs were added to the Nicene Creed to reinforce the decisions of Nicaea. It was this version of the Nicene Creed (including an affirmation of the divinity of the Holy Spirit) which is the version still used today in churches all over the world; hence it is more properly called the 'Niceno-Constantinopolitan Creed'.

That is all we need to know for our purposes in this book but it is interesting to note that the story of the Nicene Creed did not end with Constantinople. Much later the Western Church added to the creed the Latin word *filioque* (meaning 'and from the Son'). This clause asserted that the Holy Spirit proceeds not only from the Father but also from the Son. This was first added to the Western version of the creed probably in 589 by the Council of Toledo and was one of the reasons for the great schism in 1054 between the Eastern and the Western Churches, the only major split in Christianity before the Reformation.

Conclusion

After many years of biblical studies, doctrinal discussions and facing up to heresy, the church had come to a settled position at the Council of Nicaea regarding the relationship between the Father and the Son, with the recognition that Jesus was God and man at the same time. As we shall see in the next chapter, however, this led to many more years of doctrinal struggle as the church sought to answer difficult questions which arose from this shared conviction.

5

The Hypostatic Union

Introduction

In this chapter, we come to one of the most difficult issues in any study of the person of Christ, namely, how can Jesus be God and man at the same time? In chapter two we looked at the Scriptures which teach the real divinity or deity of Jesus. We saw on that occasion the clear and compelling evidence that Jesus Christ is God, the Second Person of the Trinity. Then, in chapter three, we considered the humanity of Jesus and we saw that his was a real humanity, like ours in every respect apart from the fact that he did not sin. In chapter four we looked at the inter-Trinitarian relationships and laid out some core theological truths, not least that Jesus Christ is both God and man. Now in this chapter we face a problem, namely, how do we put all of this together? How can Jesus be human and divine at the same time and how can we express this without weakening either his humanity or his divinity?

Having already explored the scriptural passages concerning Jesus' humanity and those concerning his divinity, this chapter will have a different structure from the earlier chapters. We shall begin by describing what theologians call the 'hypostatic union' and then proceed to the historical and theological debates, to demonstrate the process which led to this Christological expression.

The hypostatic union

The doctrine of the hypostatic union is the church's answer to the question as to how Jesus Christ can be God and man at the same time. More particularly, it seeks to describe how his two natures (human and divine) relate to one another in the one person. John Murray sums up the problem well:

The proposition 'God became man' could convey the thought of kenosis, subtraction, or divestiture; that the Son of God ceased to be what he was and exchanged divine identity for human; that divine attributes, prerogatives, and activities were surrendered, or at least suspended, in order that the human might be real and active. The various statements of Scripture are eloquent to the exclusion of such a conception.[1]

The word 'kenosis' which Murray uses here comes from the Greek word εϲκένωσεν used in Philippians 2:7, which is translated as 'emptied' in some English versions of the Bible. Some scholars have argued that the use of this word means that Jesus 'emptied' himself of his deity and became only a human being, so that Jesus only had one nature (human) and not two. Others have argued that, at the incarnation, the Son of God retained his divine nature but divested himself of some (or all) of his divine attributes. Yet others have argued that what was lost at the incarnation was the 'consciousness' of the divine, so that Jesus only had a human consciousness. These various 'kenotic' theories have largely been rejected by the church because they all undermine the key teaching that Jesus Christ was one person with two natures and that these natures (human and divine) were not undermined or compromised by their union in the one person of the Son of God.[2]

The church came to believe, at a very early stage in its life, that the Second Person of the Trinity, the Son of God, at a particular point in space and time, took to himself a human nature and was thus incarnated as Jesus of Nazareth, without ceasing to be God. This Jesus was both God and man, the reality of his divinity not being diminished or damaged by his humanity and the reality of his humanity being in no way compromised or undermined by its relation to his divinity. In other words, the eternal Son of God became a man, through being born of Mary. The eternal Son of God (the Second Person of the Trinity) did not take over an existing human being but rather, the person of the eternal Son, who already had a divine nature, took a human nature and he (the eternal Son) was thereafter one 'person' with two natures.

---

[1] John Murray, *Collected Writings* (Edinburgh: Banner of Truth, 1977), vol. 2, pp. 135–6.

[2] For further discussion of this 'kenosis-Christology' see G.C. Berkouwer, *The Person of Christ* (Grand Rapids, MI: Eerdmans, 1954), pp. 27–31.

Historical and theological debate

As we saw in the last chapter, at the Council of Nicaea in AD 325 it had been affirmed that Jesus Christ was God and also that Jesus Christ was man. This statement led to considerable theological debate in the ensuing years as to how this was possible, before the 'hypostatic union' was affirmed as the orthodox position of the church.

Between Nicaea and Chalcedon

Now one might have expected that, following upon the Council of Nicaea, the key theological issues had been settled but it was not so.[3] Part of the problem which contributed to the Christological battles which followed was the fact that there were two rival theological schools at work and they had different emphases. The Alexandrians were concerned to emphasize the unity of Christ whereas the Antiochenes wanted to stress the distinctness of the two natures of Christ. The fact that Jesus was both God and man had been agreed but beyond that there was no agreement. There was now a new question to be answered: How can Jesus be God and man at the same time? To that question there was a variety of answers, three of which were ultimately rejected as heretical.

Apollinaris

Apollinaris argued that the divine *logos* took the place of Christ's mind or spirit. This meant that Christ had no human spirit or human mind. The problem with this solution was that it essentially denied the incarnation. If the *logos* simply took the place of the human mind or spirit then you cannot say that the *logos* became flesh. The church rejected the solution offered by Apollinaris at the Council of Constantinople in 381 but did not offer an alternative. The question still remained: Precisely how are the divine and the human related in the person of Jesus Christ?

---

[3] For a more detailed study of the period between Nicaea to Chalcedon, see J.N.D. Kelly, *Early Christian Doctrines*, pp. 280–343; and Frances M. Young, *From Nicaea to Chalcedon* (London: SCM, 1983).

Nestorius

Nestorius was another to offer a solution. He was reputed to have argued that Christ was two persons: a divine person and a human person. Nestorius was attacked by Cyril, Bishop of Alexandria, who believed and taught that Christ was one person with two natures, one human and one divine. At the request of Cyril, the emperor called a council of the church in 431, the Council of Ephesus. At this council Nestorius was condemned. Many scholars now believe that this judgement was unfair and that the heresy was really created by the followers of Nestorius and not by Nestorius himself. As Alan Richardson says, '[Nestorius] used a word for "nature" which the Alexandrians now used only for "person" in the sense of the Person of Christ. When, therefore, he intended to speak of the two natures or aspects of Christ (divine and human), he was understood to mean that Christ was two persons.'[4]

Whether or not he himself was to blame, however, the heresy of Nestorianism did exist and required a response. Cyril provided this, although his motives have been questioned.[5]

Eutyches

A third person to come forward with a proposed solution to the problem was Eutyches. He argued that Christ had two natures prior to the incarnation but at the incarnation the divine nature swallowed up the human nature and so Christ only had a divine nature. His body, argued Eutyches, was a divine body and not like ours at all.

Once again the situation was complicated by a dispute between Alexandria and Constantinople for control of the Eastern Church. Dioscorus was Bishop of Alexandria and Flavian was Bishop of Constantinople. Dioscorus supported Eutyches. Flavian held a synod in 448 which condemned this heresy. The emperor called a synod in 449, at which the other party were in control and Eutyches was affirmed. Indeed, violence broke out and Flavian died later of injuries received! The whole church was appalled at these events. The Bishop

---

[4] A. Richardson, *Creeds in the Making* (London: SCM, 1967), pp. 77–8.

[5] As the bishop of Alexandria, it has been sugested that he was principally concerned to establish himself as the sole leader of the church. The See of Constantinople, held by Nestorious, provided the only credible challenge to Alexandria in the East at this time.

of Rome excommunicated Dioscorus and when a new emperor, Marcian, came to the throne in 450 he called a council of the church. This met at Chalcedon in 451.

The Council of Chalcedon

About four hundred and fifty delegates attended the Council of Chalcedon in 451.[6] The council covered many topics but the central issue concerned the person of Christ. The Council of Nicaea had said that Jesus was both God and man. The Council of Chalcedon now had to take this further and decide how this was possible, especially in response to the various suggestions which had been offered and rejected during the period leading up to Chalcedon. Many of the statements in the final report of the council are taken from earlier conciliar decisions, or are written in response to views which the Council of Chalcedon itself regarded as heretical.

The Christology of Chalcedon

The two great influences upon the Council of Chalcedon were Cyril of Alexandria and Pope Leo the Great. There are regular references in the Acts of the Council of Chalcedon to 'the blessed Cyril' or 'Cyril of blessed memory'. The two letters of Cyril (to Nestorius and to John of Antioch) and the *Tome* of Leo were all read at Session II of the council. Leo's *Tome*, in particular, summed up the key issues and received the support of the council.

After much debate, a formula was arrived at called the Definition of Faith, now commonly known as the Chalcedonian Definition. Here is the statement on the person of Christ:

> Following the holy Fathers we teach with one voice that the Son [of God] and our Lord Jesus Christ is to be confessed as one and the same [Person], that he is perfect in Godhead and perfect in manhood, very God and very man, of a reasonable soul and [human] body consisting, consubstantial with the Father as touching his Godhead, and consubstantial with us as

---

[6] For a study of Chalcedon see H.R. Macintosh, *The Doctrine of the Person of Jesus Christ* (Edinburgh: T&T Clark, 1937), pp. 196–222; R.V. Sellers, *The Council of Chalcedon: A Historical and Doctrinal Survey* (London: SPCK, 1961); Gerald Bray, *Creeds, Councils and Christ* (Fearn: Mentor, 1997), pp. 144–71.

touching his manhood; made in all things like unto us, sin only excepted; begotten of his Father before the worlds according to his Godhead; but in these last days for us men and for our salvation born [into the world] of the Virgin Mary, the Mother of God according to his manhood. This one and the same Jesus Christ, the only-begotten Son [of God] must be confessed to be in two natures, unconfusedly, immutably, indivisibly, inseparably [united], and that without the distinction of natures being taken away by such union, but rather the peculiar property of each nature being preserved and being united in one Person and subsistence, not separated or divided into two persons, but one and the same Son and only-begotten, God the Word, our Lord Jesus Christ, as the Prophets of old time have spoken concerning him, and as the Lord Jesus Christ hath taught us, and as the Creed of the Fathers hath delivered to us.[7]

The vital conclusion of the Council of Chalcedon, then, was that Jesus Christ has a divine nature and a human nature and that these two natures are united in the one person of Jesus Christ. Further, these natures were united without confusion, without change, without division and without separation. In this statement, the council was guarding against several errors.

Not confused or changed
It is important to affirm, as Chalcedon did, that the two natures of Christ remain as two natures. This is to guard against the view that somehow the two natures were fused together into something different, something which is neither God nor man, but an amalgam. This was the view of Eutyches. Louis Berkhof says this: 'The one divine person, who possessed a divine nature from eternity, assumed a human nature, and now has both. This must be maintained over against those who, while admitting that the divine person assumed a human nature, jeopardize the integrity of the two natures by conceiving of them as having been fused or mixed into a *tertium quid*, a sort of divine-human nature.'[8]

---

[7] Henry R. Percival, *The Seven Ecumenical Councils*, A Select Library of Nicene and Post-Nicene Fathers of the Christian Church, series 2, vol. 14 (ed. Philip Schaff and Henry Wace; Grand Rapids, MI: Eerdmans, no date), pp. 264–5.
[8] Louis Berkof, *Systematic Theology* (Edinburgh: Banner of Truth, 1971), p. 322.

Not divided or separated
On the other hand, the council had to be equally determined in affirming that the two natures were truly united together. This was to guard against those who would separate the natures. The council at this point had in mind the Nestorian view which so emphasized the distinctness of the two natures as almost to argue that Jesus Christ was two persons. Those who held this view argued that the two natures were utterly distinct and separate with no real union between them.

The theological significance of Chalcedon

Having described the process which led to the Chalcedonian Definition, we must now conclude by making three further points, to highlight the theological significance of the Definition.

The person of the logos
We must begin by noting that the one person of Jesus Christ is the person of the *logos*. It is the *logos*, the Second Person of the Trinity, who is the subject of the incarnation. The human nature of Christ is not a person. Rather the divine *logos*, who already had a divine nature, took to himself a human nature and united the two natures in his one person. That is to say, the *logos* did not take to himself a human 'person' but a human nature. The human nature of Christ does not have an independent 'subject' controlling it other than the *logos*.

This led theologians to say that the human nature of Christ was 'impersonal'. They called this the *anhypostasia*, by which they meant that the human nature of Christ does not have a 'human person' as its subject (only the person of the *logos*) and therefore it is impersonal. Some were unhappy with this notion, believing that it did not do full justice to the human nature in its relation to the *logos*. For that reason, some have used the term *enhypostasia*. Donald Macleod sums up the way in which this term is used: 'The import of *enhypostatos* is that the human nature of Christ, although not itself an individual, is individualised as the human nature of the Son of God. It does not, for a single instant, exist as *anhypostatos* or non-personal. As embryo, foetus, infant, child and man it is *hypostatos* in the Second Person of the Trinity.'[9]

---

[9] Donald Macleod, *The Person of Christ* (Leicester: IVP, 1988), p. 202.

The communio idiomatum
There are also practical issues which flow out of the Chalcedonian
Definition. For example, can we say that in his divine nature Christ is
omniscient but in his human nature he is not? Different solutions
have been proposed to solve this problem. The Lutheran Church has
always held to what is called the *communicatio idiomatum*. This means
that the properties of the divine nature are transferred (communicat-
ed) to the human nature. John Murray affirms the truth which the
Lutherans are anxious to preserve, namely, that 'whatever can be
predicated of either nature can be predicated of the person'[10] but he
rejects the Lutheran way of expressing this. Rather he argues for a
communio idiomatum. He writes, 'The Reformed view is rather that
what is true of either nature is true of the person, and the person may
be designated in terms of one nature when what is predicated is true
only in virtue of the other.'[11]

The last Adam
These last two points may seem somewhat abstruse and purely technical, although they are important. We must conclude, however,
with a matter which takes us to the very heart of the significance of
the hypostatic union, namely, the affirmation that because Christ
was both God and man, he was able to serve as Mediator and
Saviour.

God, as we saw in an earlier chapter, entered into a relationship
with the first Adam, promising that death would follow disobedience
with the implication that life would follow obedience. Adam disobeyed, bringing death upon himself and the entire human race. God
did not thereby abandon the human race; rather he entered into
another relationship with the human race, this time in Jesus Christ.
Since Jesus Christ is man, he could be our representative; since he is
God, he could offer a worthy sacrifice. Here, then, is the ultimate significance of the hypostatic union: the death of the God-man as our
representative and substitute.

In affirming the hypostatic union, we bear witness to the triumph
of Christ, the last Adam, who has accomplished salvation on our
behalf. This was well expressed by Cardinal John Henry Newman
(1801–90) in his great hymn:

---

[10] John Murray, *Collected Writings of John Murray, vol. 2: Systematic Theology*
(Edinburgh: The Banner of Truth Trust, 1977), p. 140.
[11] Murray, *Systematic Theology*, p. 140.

O loving wisdom of our God!
When all was sin and shame,
A second Adam to the fight
And to the rescue came.

O wisest love! that flesh and blood,
Which did in Adam fail,
Should strive afresh against the foe,
Should strive and should prevail.

Post-Chalcedonian developments

We have seen the way in which part of the doctrine of the person of Christ was established at Nicaea and we have seen what was later clarified at Chalcedon. But the matter was not yet completely finished. The result of the Council of Chalcedon was agreement on the doctrine of the person of Christ. It was not, however, unanimous. One of the sad results of the council was that the Egyptian and Syrian Churches seceded from the Catholic Church because they held a different view of the person of Christ. They believed in what has come to be called 'monophysitism'. This view taught that Christ had only one nature, a divine nature. Various attempts were made to heal this breach but they failed.

Part of the reason for the monophysite position was a mistaken understanding of, and misplaced loyalty to, Cyril of Alexandria, who succeeded his uncle Theophilus as Bishop of Alexandria in AD 412. Cyril was a very gifted and profound scholar and a fine theologian and he owed a considerable debt to Athanasius whose theology he accepted and carried forward. On one point everyone is agreed: he had a deep and thorough grasp of the Scriptures, and he brought this knowledge of Scripture to bear on the theological debates in which he was involved. He was well established by the year AD 428 when Nestorius became Bishop of Constantinople. His battle against Nestorius and against the Nestorian heresy occupied the greater part of his time and energy for the greater part of his life. In opposition to Nestorius, Cyril placed great stress on the unity of Christ and he used the expression 'one nature' to refer to Christ. This view was deeply imbedded in the Alexandrian approach to Christology before Chalcedon.

Cyril's theology, however, was quite in accord with Chalcedon and when he and other Alexandrians used the expression 'one nature' to speak of Christ it was because the difference between 'person' and 'nature' had still not been clarified. He meant one 'self-determining being'.[12] Those who mistakenly sought to promote this 'one nature' theology after Chalcedon also believed that Christ only had one will; hence they became known as 'monothelites'. This view was condemned at the Lateran Council in AD 649. This was not one of the seven ecumenical councils but the condemnation was repeated in AD 680 at the Council of Constantinople, which was.

Scripture and tradition

It is perhaps appropriate at this stage in the book to ask why the church places such weight on the decisions of councils such as Nicaea and Chalcedon. After all, the Chalcedonian Definition, although important, does not have the authority which we accord to the voice of God speaking by his Holy Spirit in Scripture.

The church has almost universally accepted the key decisions of the main ecumenical councils and we do well to think carefully before rejecting such time-honoured and respected formulations, but they do not have final authority. When Robert Reymond rejected aspects of conciliar teaching on the Trinity in his volume of systematic theology,[13] there were wide and sustained protests and condemnations. Those who objected to his theological conclusions had, of course, every right to argue with him on the detail. What was inappropriate for Protestant theologians was the argument that he had no right to challenge, or disagree with, such august bodies as the councils of Nicaea or Chalcedon.

This identifies the need for an evangelical theology of tradition. Tradition must not be regarded as an authority to be put alongside Scripture, as in Roman Catholicism, or as a body of church teaching which includes Scripture, as in Eastern Orthodoxy, but it must be recognized as a vital strand of our theology. We are not the first Christians to reflect on Scripture and we should value the work of those who have gone before us. In the Reformed tradition of Protestantism we value certain confessional statements to the point where we use them as an entry test for ordinands and as a theological canon for purposes

[12] Bray, Creeds, *Councils and Christ*, p. 150.
[13] Robert L. Reymond, *A New Systematic Theology of the Christian Faith* (Nashville, TN: Thomas Nelson, 1998).

of discipline. This is effectively to have a theology of tradition because we are elevating a human statement to the point where we require affirmation of it as well as of Scripture. This has always been the case in the Reformed tradition. As Herman Bavinck has shown us, the Reformers did not reject tradition *per se* but only bad tradition![14]

Conclusion

The church, through this great Council of Chalcedon, taught that, at the incarnation, the Second Person of the Trinity, God the Son (or *logos*), took to himself a human nature and was born as Jesus of Nazareth. The Son of God thus had two natures, one divine and one human, both of which were subsumed under the one acting subject. From the biblical evidence presented in the earlier chapters, we can affirm that there is nothing in the Chalcedonian Definition which is contrary to Scripture. Certainly the Definition goes well beyond Scripture in its use of language and terminology and makes distinctions which the church had yet to make when the New Testament was completed. Nevertheless, the New Testament is clearly set on a trajectory which is perfectly in keeping with Chalcedon.

In addition to this, the council reaffirmed the decisions of previous councils, not least the ones at Nicaea (325) and Constantinople (381). In other words, the Definition of Faith was not viewed as a replacement for the Niceno-Constantinopolitan Creed but as a spelling out of its central tenets and an expansion of its key themes, answering some new questions. The Chalcedonian Definition remains today the classic statement on Christological matters and has been accepted historically by virtually all churches, whether Orthodox, Roman Catholic or Protestant.

This doctrine of the hypostatic union is complex and requires us to walk very carefully in a minefield of potential errors and heresies. In one sense, this is a mystery which we will never fully comprehend but nevertheless we are required to state what we believe God has revealed to us of this mystery. The Council of Chalcedon did not claim to have fully understood or 'settled' the mystery of the hypostatic union but, in seeking to understand and expound the Scriptures, it laid down parameters for the church. We can do no more than that.

---

[14] Herman Bavinck, *Reformed Dogmatics, vol. 1: Prolegomena* (Grand Rapids, MI: Baker, 2003), p. 493.

6

Christ's Exaltation

Introduction

In biblical studies it is normal to speak about Christ's incarnation, his life of obedience and his death on the cross as his 'humiliation'. Then, when we turn to speak of his resurrection, ascension, heavenly session and second coming, we call it his 'exaltation'. The expression is found in Philippians 2, a passage that we have turned to several times already:

> [Christ], being in very nature God, did not consider equality with God something to be grasped, but made himself nothing, taking the very nature of a servant, being made in human likeness. And being found in appearance as a man, he humbled himself and became obedient to death – even death on a cross! Therefore God exalted him to the highest place and gave him the name that is above every name, that at the name of Jesus every knee should bow, in heaven and on earth and under the earth, and every tongue confess that Jesus Christ is Lord, to the glory of God the Father.

As we consider that exaltation, we break it up into its five constitutive parts: first, the resurrection; second, the ascension; third, the heavenly session; fourth, the second coming; and fifth, the judgement.

The resurrection

The resurrection of Jesus Christ is not a legend or a myth; it is historical fact. At a certain point in time, in a particular geographical location, Jesus of Nazareth was raised from the dead. He then appeared to his friends and disciples over a forty-day period.

Part of the reason for speaking so confidently is because the resurrection was central to the preaching of the early church. Many people today, if asked to summarize the gospel, would point to the cross and say, 'Christ died for our sins' but, in fact, for the earliest Christian preachers, the resurrection was critical. We see that in Acts 4:33: 'With great power the apostles continued to testify to the resurrection of the Lord Jesus, and much grace was upon them all.' Then we see it again in Acts 17:18: 'A group of Epicurean and Stoic philosophers began to dispute with him. Some of them asked, "What is this babbler trying to say?" Others remarked, "He seems to be advocating foreign gods." They said this because Paul was preaching the good news about Jesus and the resurrection.' Paul emphasized the resurrection because he viewed it as a declaration of the identity of Jesus. As we read in Romans 1:4, 'who through the Spirit of holiness was declared with power to be the Son of God, by his resurrection from the dead: Jesus Christ our Lord.' That is to say, it was God's vindication of Jesus, the proof to everyone that God had accepted the sacrificial offering which he made on behalf of sinners.

The weight of significance placed on the resurrection is also evident when the early church came to choose a disciple to replace Judas Iscariot. The job description was very clear, as we see from Acts 1:21–22: 'Therefore it is necessary to choose one of the men who have been with us the whole time the Lord Jesus went in and out among us, beginning from John's baptism to the time when Jesus was taken up from us. For one of these must become a witness with us of his resurrection.' The new apostle was to be a witness to the resurrection.

Why was the resurrection given such a significant place? It was because of the apostles' conviction that without the resurrection there is no salvation. The classic statement of this comes in 1 Corinthians 15:12–20, where Paul states that if Jesus Christ did not rise from the dead, then there is no forgiveness of sins and those who have died are lost:

> But if it is preached that Christ has been raised from the dead, how can some of you say that there is no resurrection of the dead? If there is no resurrection of the dead, then not even Christ has been raised. And if Christ has not been raised, our preaching is useless and so is your faith. More than that, we are then found to be false witnesses about God, for we have testified about God that he raised Christ from the dead. But he did not raise him if in fact the dead are not raised. For if the dead are not raised, then Christ has not been raised either. And if Christ has not

been raised, your faith is futile; you are still in your sins. Then those
also who have fallen asleep in Christ are lost. If only for this life we
have hope in Christ, we are to be pitied more than all men.

Paul is addressing these words to those who did not believe that Jesus
had been raised from the dead. The message is simple: if there was no
resurrection, then there is no gospel, no forgiveness, no salvation and
no hope. He also expounds this relationship between resurrection and
justification in Romans 4:25: 'He was delivered over to death for our
sins and was raised to life for our justification.'

Paul was not alone in viewing the resurrection in this way. Peter
gave the same high place to the resurrection, as we see in 1 Peter
1:3–9: 'Praise be to the God and Father of our Lord Jesus Christ! In
his great mercy he has given us new birth into a living hope
through the resurrection of Jesus Christ from the dead . . .' Clearly,
then, for the apostles, the resurrection is critical for human salvation.

The ascension

The ascension is described in the last few words of Luke's gospel,
Luke 24:50–53: 'When he had led them out to the vicinity of Bethany,
he lifted up his hands and blessed them. While he was blessing them,
he left them and was taken up into heaven. Then they worshipped
him and returned to Jerusalem with great joy. And they stayed con-
tinually at the temple, praising God.' It is then described more fully in
Acts 1:9–11:

> After he said this, he was taken up before their very eyes, and a cloud
> hid him from their sight. They were looking intently up into the sky
> as he was going, when suddenly two men dressed in white stood
> beside them. 'Men of Galilee,' they said, 'why do you stand here look-
> ing into the sky? This same Jesus, who has been taken from you into
> heaven, will come back in the same way you have seen him go into
> heaven.'

For the disciples, this was the parting of the ways. Jesus had been
appearing to his disciples and others after the resurrection for forty
days but now he was returning to his Father. It is difficult to understand what actually happened. How could the God-man, the one who

had both a divine nature and a human nature, ascend into heaven? It is a mystery but the teaching of Scripture is clear: the Son of God was taken up into heaven without ceasing to have two natures. That is to say, there is a person with a human nature in heaven at the right hand of the Father. Christ has completed the work of salvation and made a way for human beings to enter into a right relationship with God. He has now entered into the glory which he had with the Father before the world began.

The heavenly session

When we speak of the heavenly session, we are referring to the fact that Jesus is now seated (hence the word 'session') at the right hand of God. We read of this in Ephesians 1:19 – 2:1:

> . . . That power is like the working of his mighty strength, which he exerted in Christ when he raised him from the dead and seated him at his right hand in the heavenly realms, far above all rule and authority, power and dominion, and every title that can be given, not only in the present age but also in the one to come. And God placed all things under his feet and appointed him to be head over everything for the church, which is his body, the fulness of him who fills everything in every way.

It is also there in the next chapter, in Ephesians 2:6: 'And God raised us up with Christ and seated us with him in the heavenly realms in Christ Jesus'. Similarly, Paul mentions it in Colossians 3:1: 'Since, then, you have been raised with Christ, set your hearts on things above, where Christ is seated at the right hand of God.' One point to notice here is that not only has Christ been seated at the right hand of God but, because we are spiritually united to him, Paul can say that we too have been caught up together with him.

If we ask what Christ is doing during this period of heavenly session, then the answer is that he is acting on behalf of his people. The most significant element of this continuing work is the intercession he offers on behalf of his people, as we shall see in the next chapter.

These references indicate that Christ's heavenly session marks the continuation of his priestly ministry of intercession. The implication is that he will do this until he returns.

The second coming

The doctrine of the second coming of Christ has been confused and over-dramatized by speculative and indulgent theories based on one or two verses of Scripture, while quite ignoring many less obscure and less difficult passages. A basic principle of biblical studies (especially relevant to this area) is that difficult and unclear passages of Scripture, especially those which are allegorical or symbolic, must be understood in the light of those passages which are clear and unmistakable. Most of the confused and even heretical teaching on this subject has come about because people ignored this and tried to build a doctrine of the 'last things' on the basis of passages which, at best, are capable of sustaining several interpretations.

The New Testament clearly teaches that Jesus Christ will return to this earth one day. In what is called the 'little apocalypse' of Mark 13:26–27, we read this: 'At that time men will see the Son of Man coming in clouds with great power and glory. And he will send his angels and gather his elect from the four winds, from the ends of the earth to the ends of the heavens.' Similarly, Jesus told his disciples that he would come back for them, in John 14:2–3: 'In my Father's house are many rooms; if it were not so, I would have told you. I am going there to prepare a place for you. And if I go and prepare a place for you, I will come back and take you to be with me that you also may be where I am.' It is there in the words of the two men dressed in white who speak to the disciples after the ascension, as recorded in Acts 1:11: '"Men of Galilee," they said, "why do you stand here looking into the sky? This same Jesus, who has been taken from you into heaven, will come back in the same way you have seen him go into heaven."'

This assurance that Christ will return to earth one day became a feature of the preaching of the early church, for example in Peter's preaching after the healing of the crippled beggar outside the Temple, of which we read in Acts 3:19–21: 'Repent, then, and turn to God, so that your sins may be wiped out, that times of refreshing may come from the Lord, and that he may send the Christ, who has been appointed for you – even Jesus. He must remain in heaven until the time comes for God to restore everything, as he promised long ago through his holy prophets.' There are also references which imply the second coming, by referring to the fact that Jesus will judge the world. We hear this from Peter in Acts 10:42 and from Paul in Acts 17:31.

Each of the writers of the New Testament epistles makes reference to the second coming of Jesus. Paul, speaking of Jesus in 1 Corinthians

15:23, refers to the time 'when he comes'. Paul's most explicit teaching on the subject is to be found in 1 Thessalonians 4:13–17:

> Brothers, we do not want you to be ignorant about those who fall asleep, or to grieve like the rest of men, who have no hope. We believe that Jesus died and rose again and so we believe that God will bring with Jesus those who have fallen asleep in him. According to the Lord's own word, we tell you that we who are still alive, who are left till the coming of the Lord, will certainly not precede those who have fallen asleep. For the Lord himself will come down from heaven, with a loud command, with the voice of the archangel and with the trumpet call of God, and the dead in Christ will rise first. After that, we who are still alive and are left will be caught up together with them in the clouds to meet the Lord in the air. And so we will be with the Lord for ever.

The writer to the Hebrews adds his own reflection in Hebrews 9:28: 'Christ was sacrificed once to take away the sins of many people; and he will appear a second time, not to bear sin, but to bring salvation to those who are waiting for him.' James, in his letter, tells people to be patient, 'until the Lord's coming' (5:7). Peter speaks of the 'day of the Lord' to refer to the second coming of Christ and the judgement associated with it (2 Peter 3:8–13). Finally, the apostle John looks forward to the second coming of Jesus, as described in 1 John 3:2: 'Dear friends, now we are children of God, and what we will be has not yet been made known. But we know that when he appears, we shall be like him, for we shall see him as he is.'

Certain aspects of this second coming are described in Scripture. We are told that it will be sudden and unexpected (Matthew 24:37–44) and that it will mark the end of time (1 Corinthians 15:24). As to when it will happen, the date is not known by anyone (Matthew 24:36).

The judgement

One thing is clear from Scripture, namely, that the return of Christ will usher in the Day of Judgement. We see this in Matthew 25:31–33: 'When the Son of Man comes in his glory, and all the angels with him, he will sit on his throne in heavenly glory. All the nations will be gathered before him, and he will separate the people one from another as a shepherd separates the sheep from the goats. He will put the sheep on his right and the goats on his left.' The identity of this coming one is not in doubt: it is the Lord Jesus Christ. He is the 'Son of Man' (the name Jesus used to describe himself) but he is sitting on a throne and, as verse 34 says, he is the King. As King and Judge, he oversees a great separation and the basis on which this judgement is made is spelled out in great detail:

> Then the King will say to those on his right, 'Come, you who are blessed by my Father; take your inheritance, the kingdom prepared for you since the creation of the world. For I was hungry and you gave me something to eat, I was thirsty and you gave me something to drink, I was a stranger and you invited me in, I needed clothes and you clothed me, I was sick and you looked after me, I was in prison and you came to visit me.' Then the righteous will answer him, 'Lord, when did we see you hungry and feed you, or thirsty and give you something to drink? When did we see you a stranger and invite you in, or needing clothes and clothe you? When did we see you sick or in prison and go to visit you?' The King will reply, 'I tell you the truth, whatever you did for one of the least of these brothers of mine, you did for me.' Then he will say to those on his left, 'Depart from me, you who are cursed, into the eternal fire prepared for the devil and his angels. For I was hungry and you gave me nothing to eat, I was thirsty and you gave me nothing to drink, I was a stranger and you did not invite me in, I needed clothes and you did not clothe me, I was sick and in prison and you did not look after me.' They also will answer, 'Lord, when did we see you hungry or thirsty or a stranger or needing clothes or sick or in prison, and did not help you?' He will reply, 'I tell you the truth, whatever you did not do for one of the least of these, you did not do for me.' Then they will go away to eternal punishment, but the righteous to eternal life.

Those who are welcomed into the heavenly kingdom are those who have fed the hungry, clothed the naked, looked after the sick and visited those in prison. For many people, this teaching has posed a problem. Many Christians, if asked about the qualifications for getting into heaven, will talk about faith in Christ, about being 'born again' or whatever. Yet there is other teaching, similar in nature to these words of Jesus in Matthew 25. For example, in Matthew 16:27 we read this: 'For the Son of Man is going to come in his Father's glory with his angels, and then he will reward each person according to what he has done.' Then there is 2 Corinthians 5:10: 'For we must all appear before the judgment seat of Christ, that each one may receive what is due to him for the things done while in the body, whether good or bad.' There is also the famous passage from Revelation 20:11–15:

> Then I saw a great white throne and him who was seated on it. Earth and sky fled from his presence, and there was no place for them. And I saw the dead, great and small, standing before the throne, and books were opened. Another book was opened, which is the book of life. The dead were judged according to what they had done as recorded in the books. The sea gave up the dead that were in it, and death and Hades gave up the dead that were in them, and each person was judged according to what he had done. Then death and Hades were thrown into the lake of fire. The lake of fire is the second death. If anyone's name was not found written in the book of life, he was thrown into the lake of fire.

How can we reconcile this teaching about salvation being determined by human action, with the teaching in Scripture that salvation is by grace through faith? Part of the problem lies in the fact that, at face value, it seems as if there is a contradiction in the Bible between what James says and what Paul says. In Romans 4:1–3, Paul says, 'What then shall we say that Abraham, our forefather, discovered in this matter? If, in fact, Abraham was justified by works, he had something to boast about – but not before God. What does the Scripture say? "Abraham believed God, and it was credited to him as righteousness."' Compare that with James 2:21–24: 'Was not our ancestor Abraham considered righteous for what he did when he offered his son Isaac on the altar? You see that his faith and his actions were working together, and his faith was made complete by what he did. And the scripture was fulfilled that says, "Abraham believed God, and it was credited to him as righteousness," and he was called God's friend. You see that a person is justified by what he does and not by faith alone.'

The answer lies in properly understanding the relation between what you believe and what you do, between faith and action. Paul is teaching us very properly that salvation is by faith, but James is teaching us that true faith shows itself in practical action. This connection between faith and works is really based upon the connection between the doctrines of justification and sanctification. We are justified by faith but this immediately leads to sanctification by the Holy Spirit. It is not possible to have one without the other: if there is no sanctification, then there has been no justification. Faith without works is dead.

It is important that we understand what is being said here. God does not say, 'You have become a Christian; therefore be good.' Rather he says, 'Since you have become a Christian, you will be good.' It is a description rather than an injunction. In James 2:14–26, James is dealing with someone who is claiming to be a Christian but where there is no evidence to support the claim. Essentially James tells us that such a situation is unthinkable. If Christ has entered a person's life then there will be results. If a person has undergone new birth then new life will follow. In other words, Christian living is the fundamental test of Christian discipleship and Christian faith. If the root of the matter is in us at all, then we will give evidence of that by our works. New life is the primary evidence of new birth.

We must not try to 'solve' this dichotomy between faith and works but instead we must recognize its importance. Christians have sometimes tended to emphasize one element of this truth or the other. That is to say, they argue that salvation is by faith or that it is by works. On the one hand it is possible so to emphasize the Pauline teaching that Christianity becomes a religion of words and doctrines with practical Christian living written off as the 'social gospel'. On the other hand, it is possible so to emphasize the teaching of James that Christianity is reduced to social work and soup kitchens or to peace and justice. Only when the two emphases are locked together can the Christian faith be whole and complete.

We are justified by faith, but we prove our faith by the way that we live. See, for example, Paul's words in Acts 26:20: 'First to those in Damascus, then to those in Jerusalem and in all Judea, and to the Gentiles also, I preached that they should repent and turn to God and prove their repentance by their deeds.' When we read Matthew 25 and the words of Jesus about the Day of Judgement we must not misunderstand them. Jesus is not saying that salvation is to be obtained by good works; he is saying that good works are one evidence that new birth and new life are present in the life of the believer.

Death and resurrection

With all of this in mind, we can now ask the question about what will happen from the point of death until we reach our eternal destination. We can do no better than consider the summary found in the *Westminster Confession of Faith*, chapter 32, section 1:

The bodies of men, after death, return to dust, and see corruption; but their souls (which neither die nor sleep), having an immortal subsistence, immediately return to God who gave them. The souls of the righteous, being then made perfect in holiness, are received into the highest heavens, where they behold the face of God in light and glory, waiting for the full redemption of their bodies; and the souls of the wicked are cast into hell, where they remain in torments and utter darkness, reserved to the judgment of the great day. Besides these two places for souls separated from their bodies, the Scripture acknowledgeth none.

You will notice that there are four key points being made in that quotation. First there will be a division of soul and body (Luke 23:43; Ecclesiastes 12:7). Second, the body will return to dust (Genesis 3:19; Acts 13:36). Third, the souls of the righteous go immediately to paradise (Luke 23:43 cf. 1 Corinthians 15:18; 2 Corinthians 5:8; Philippians 1:23). Fourth, the souls of the wicked go to Hades/hell (Luke 16:19–31; 1 Peter 3:18–20).

Sometimes there is confusion over Hades and hell. In this regard a quotation from T.C. Hammond, a great evangelical scholar of a previous generation, might be helpful. Hammond says that heaven and hell are used only as a description of what happens after the judgement whereas 'Hades' and 'paradise' are used for the intermediate period.[1]

We can now read on in the *Westminster Confession of Faith* chapter 32, sections 2 and 3:

At the last day, such as are found alive shall not die, but be changed: and all the dead shall be raised up with the selfsame bodies, and none other, although with different qualities, which shall be united again to their souls forever.

The bodies of the unjust shall, by the power of Christ, be raised to dishonour; the bodies of the just, by his Spirit, unto honour, and be made conformable to his own glorious body.

There are three things here of particular note: first, there is to be a general resurrection of the dead (John 5:25–29; 6:39–40; Romans 8:23;

---

[1] T.C. Hammond, *In Understanding Be Men* (ed. D.F. Wright; Leicester: IVP, rev. edn, 1968), p. 188.

1 Corinthians 15:42–44). Second, believers will be given 'resurrection bodies' appropriate to the new environment, just as Jesus' resurrection body demonstrated continuity and discontinuity. Third, believers shall be like Christ (1 John 3:2). Two passages draw the threads of this together: 1 Thessalonians 4:13 – 5:11 and 1 Corinthians 15:51ff.

With all of this in mind, we can return to the theme of the Day of Judgement. The key verses here are Hebrews 9:27–28: 'Just as man is destined to die once, and after that to face judgement, so Christ was sacrificed once to take away the sins of many people; and he will appear a second time, not to bear sin, but to bring salvation to those who are waiting for him.' This judgement, then, will accompany the coming of Christ. The judging will be done by Jesus Christ, appointed by the Father to this purpose (Acts 17:31). All will be judged, even Christians (2 Corinthians 5:10), but we should have no fear because there is now no condemnation for those who are in Christ Jesus (Romans 8:1). In this judgement there will be reward and loss, that is to say, the value of Christian service will be judged (1 Corinthians 3:10–15).

For the believer that Day of Judgement is filled with hope. As we read in 1 Corinthians 2:9–10, '"No eye has seen, no ear has heard, no mind has conceived what God has prepared for those who love him" – but God has revealed it to us by his Spirit.' Or, to put it poetically in the words of Thomas Boston (1676–1732): 'The presence and enjoyment of God and the lamb shall satisfy them with pleasures for evermore. They shall swim for ever in an ocean of joy, and every object they see shall fill them with the most ecstatic joy, which shall be ever fresh and new to them, through all the ages of eternity.'[2]

Historical and theological debate

In the modern period, it is the frankly supernatural nature of the claims regarding Jesus' resurrection, ascension, heavenly session and second coming which has drawn most criticism. Especially since the Enlightenment, scholars have simply not been prepared to accept these concepts, except in a mythological or a figurative sense.

---

[2] Samuel McMillan, ed., *The Complete Works of Thomas Boston* (London: William Tegg & Co, 1853), vol. 1, p. 15.

The Enlightenment

The origins of this approach are to be found in the Enlightenment, a period when philosophers chose to abandon any concept of external authority in decision-making and to trust in their own autonomous rationality. In exploring any subject, the authority of the state or the church or even the authority of supposed 'inspired' texts must be put to one side. The individual scholar, using reason, becomes the final arbiter of truth. Theologians followed the philosophers of the Enlightenment and brought the principles of human autonomy and the final authority of reason into Christian theology.

Historical-critical method

Parallel to this movement, and heavily dependent upon it, was the beginning of what came to be called the 'historical-critical method'. This method of studying the books which make up our Bibles began with the conviction that these books were not supernaturally given to us by God but were books like any other and so must be explored 'scientifically', in exactly the same way in which we would study any other ancient text. This method of study began with a number of significant presuppositions, not least that if an ancient book described something supernatural or miraculous, the scholar must begin with the assumption that this event did not happen historically. The method also assumed that the books under study often had multiple authors over a long period, with the later church adding significantly to the original manuscripts for its own purposes. The method taught that every passage must be understood only within its own historical, social and religious context. This meant that prophecy and messianic interpretation was largely to be rejected. If a book spoke accurately about historical events, then it was assumed that it must have been written after these events, since another presupposition is that no-one can tell what will happen in the future.

This historical-critical method of biblical exegesis seriously damaged the study of theology and especially Christology. The concepts of Jesus' pre-existence, incarnation, miraculous healings, resurrection, ascension and second coming were all regarded as mythological ideas intended to stress the significance of Jesus, while having no basis in history. The earlier scholars in this tradition, like Schleiermacher, were more restrained in their approach but scholars have become more and more radical as the years have passed.

Quest for the historical Jesus

One movement within this broad school of thought argued that we must separate the historical Jesus from the 'Christ of faith' and hence strip away all supernatural elements in order to 'find' the real Jesus. This was named the 'Quest for the Historical Jesus' in 1904 by Albert Schweitzer but was initiated much earlier by H.S. Reimarus in the eighteenth century and W. Wrede in the nineteenth century. This was the 'first' quest for the historical Jesus. Other scholars continued this work and, in the 1980s, E.P. Sanders was credited as beginning the 'third quest' for the historical Jesus. M.H. Burer sums up the historical development in this way: 'The major periods are the Old Quest, from 1778 to 1906; an interim period or "No Quest," from 1906 to 1953; the New Quest, from 1953 to the present day; and the Third Quest, from the early 1980's until the present day.'[3] Although this analysis has held sway for some time, there has recently been a significant move away from dividing the 'quests' into these periods, since it does not seem to take account of all the relevant scholarship, especially in the USA and the United Kingdom.

The Jesus Seminar

The most radical group in this 'quest' is the 'Jesus Seminar'. The work was led by Robert Funk and included notable scholars such as John Dominic Crossan. The participants used coloured beads to indicate whether or not (or how far) a particular saying of or about Jesus was authentic. Their conclusions, not surprisingly, followed upon the principles which they laid down at the beginning and which were seriously biased towards discovering a human Jesus rather than a Jesus who was the Son of God. The members of the seminar believe that Jesus was a human child, born to Mary and Joseph, and was not the incarnation of God. They reject his miracles and do not believe that he died for sinners on the cross. Their main conclusion is that Jesus was a wise man who spoke out against injustice. It should be noted, however, that conservative scholars such as N.T. Wright have also participated in the 'third quest' and have sought to respond to the more radical approaches. Wright's defence of the bodily resurrec-

---

[3] Michael H. Burer, 'A Survey of Historical Jesus Studies: From Reimarus to Wright' https://www.bible.org/article/survey-historical-jesus-studies-reimarus-wright (accessed 27 Dec. 2011).

tion of Jesus against Crossan is a case in point. A significant contribution was also made by I. Howard Marshall.[4]

Sometimes we are given the impression that a failure to accept the so-called 'scientific conclusions' of the scholars who deny the reality of incarnation, resurrection, ascension and second coming means that we are obscurantists or fundamentalists. Some will argue that, in order to be intellectually honest, convictions which involve faith and the teaching of the church should be put to one side in the search for truth. Such a view implies that the only knowledge which is real is that which comes through our senses and by rational reflection on the information so gathered. It also implies that the 'scientific' method is indeed scientific. In fact, the presuppositions on both sides have to be subject to analysis.

If, on the one hand, you begin with the presupposition that miracles do not happen and that we must reject any reference to the supernatural, then it is not surprising that you end up with a human Jesus who did not perform any miracles and was emphatically not the Son of God, a Jesus who was simply a good teacher, who challenged the establishment of his day. If, on the other hand, you begin with the presupposition that there is a God who has chosen to make himself known to the human race which he created, that he spoke authoritatively and supernaturally through prophets and apostles and that he also spoke fully and finally through Jesus Christ his Son, then you will come to quite different conclusions. Contrary to the view that the first set of presuppositions is 'scientific' and the second is not, we must respond by saying that there is a 'knowledge' which comes to us by revelation from God and through encounter with God. We might also point out the arrogance of assuming that the rational method of a human being can be the final arbiter of truth.

Scripture

The fault line in all of this is our approach to Scripture. Is Scripture the revelation of God or is it merely a collection of human writings which indicate what men and women of faith believed at different times in history? Is Scripture a description of what human beings say about God, or is it a revelation of what God says to human beings? In

---

[4] I. Howard Marshall, *I Believe in the Historical Jesus* (Grand Rapids, MI: Eerdmans, 1977).

answering these questions, it is important to stress that we can have a theological method which is 'scientific' and yet accords with the teaching of Scripture. After all, a properly scientific method is one where the method of investigation is determined by the object of study. In this case, the object of our study is God. How then should we approach Scripture?

The origin of Scripture

While fully recognizing the humanity of the biblical authors and the contextual nature of what they wrote, we affirm that Scripture has its origins in God. The apostle Paul says in 2 Timothy 3:16 that 'all Scripture is God-breathed' and the apostle Peter, in 2 Peter 1:21, says that 'men spoke from God as they were carried along by the Holy Spirit.' The conclusion we must draw from this is that the Scriptures are not simply an interesting record of what religious people have believed from time to time in the history of the Judaeo-Christian continuum; rather they have their origins in God and so carry the full authority of God as he spoke (and continues to speak) by his Spirit through the human authors.

The nature of Scripture

It follows from this conviction concerning the origins of Scripture that the Scriptures are, in the words of the *Westminster Confession of Faith*, 'the Word of God written.' The *Westminster Confession of Faith* elaborates on this view: 'The authority of the holy Scripture, for which it ought to be believed and obeyed, dependeth not upon the testimony of any man or Church, but wholly upon God (who is truth itself), the Author thereof; and therefore it is to be received, because it is the Word of God.'[5]

The interpretation of Scripture

In the Reformed tradition, following Calvin, the key to understanding and interpreting Scripture has always been to recognize the important and integral relationship between Word and Spirit. It was the Holy Spirit who brought the Scriptures into existence (origins), it was the Holy Spirit who enabled the church to recognize Scripture as

---

[5] *Westminster Confession of Faith*, ch. 1, section 4.

Scripture (canonicity), it is the Holy Spirit who helps us to understand the meaning of Scripture (illumination) and it is the Holy Spirit who enables the preaching of Scripture (empowerment). This being the case, the 'text' must be read in an attitude of prayer and worship, seeking the mind of the Holy Spirit, recognizing that the Spirit will never contradict what has been given to us in Scripture.

This means that, following the Reformers and the Reformation tradition, the Scriptures are to be interpreted using certain core methods. First, there must be an examination of the original Hebrew and Greek texts by grammatico-historical exegesis. Second, there should follow a thorough investigation of the literary, social, cultural and historical background to the text. Third, the text should be examined in context, taking account of the place of the text in the canonical book and in the Bible as a whole, seeking to understand the intention of the author and the theological structure of the argument being presented. Fourth, there ought to be a recognition that difficult passages must be read in the light of clearer passages. Fifth, like the Reformers we should begin with a commitment to the fundamental unity of Scripture as the Word of God and hence part of our interpretation will involve comparing Scripture with Scripture.

It must be recognized, of course, that even using these principles, Christians will disagree. There are many subjects on which honest and faithful exegetes have come to differing conclusions. In the New Testament, for example, there are strands of teaching on baptism, on the relation between church and state, on eschatology and many other matters, where Christians have gone to Scripture, believing it to be the Word of God, and reached contradictory positions. These are differences 'within the family' and should not bring separation of fellowship.

Conclusion

In the midst of this defence against liberal and radical interpretations of the Bible and consequent rejection of the truths of incarnation, resurrection and so on, we must not lose sight of the fact that the issues before us are not simply matters for academic debate. Among other things, in this chapter we have been discussing the resurrection and glorification of Jesus. This is vitally relevant for our own lives both now and in the future. As Christ was resurrected, so shall those who trust in him be given resurrection bodies (1 Corinthians 15:35ff.). As

Christ was glorified, so shall those who trust in him be glorified (Romans 8:30). We must not allow a biased, intellectually weak and scientifically questionable (so-called) scholarship to undermine our experience of the living and true God through his Son, Jesus Christ.

7

The Work of Christ

Introduction

In the first six chapters of this book, we have been dealing with the person of Christ and we have asked questions about his identity, about his humanity and his divinity, about where he fits into the Trinity and about the way in which his human nature and divine nature are related in the one person of the Son of God. We also considered the work of the Holy Spirit in the birth and life of Jesus and we saw both Christ's humiliation (in going down from heaven to death) and his exaltation (in going from death, through resurrection and ascension, to his place at God's right hand). In addition, we surveyed the theological development of the doctrine of the person of Christ until it was codified and almost universally accepted in the church.

We now move on to the second half of the book, as we consider the work of Christ. When we are considering the work of Christ we are focussing on what he has done for us, particularly (but not exclusively) through his death and resurrection. As indicated at the beginning of this book, there is a significant difference between the church's understanding of the person of Christ and its understanding of the work of Christ. In terms of Christology, there were various heresies and controversies which forced the church to reach a conclusion, although it was AD 451 before this conclusion was formally defined in anything like a complete state. Nevertheless, when these conclusions were reached and defined, the resulting Christology was almost universally accepted. Indeed, to this day, most Christian traditions retain the high Christology of the fifth century, including the mainstream Churches, whether Orthodox, Roman Catholic, Lutheran, Reformed, Baptist, Anglican or Methodist. Since the late seventeenth century, this Christology has been challenged (as we have seen) but these challenges have rarely impacted the dogmatic formulations of the churches.

The situation in respect of the atonement is very different. There has been no agreement among the churches, such as there was with Christology. A whole range of different theories of atonement have existed and continue to exist. Significant theological work is both necessary and long overdue. This will involve a careful listening, an openness to dialogue, a refusal to accept stereotypes, a recognition that the positions held in the sixteenth and seventeenth centuries are not necessarily the ones held today and an approach to theology which is not combative in its essential methodology. It will also recognize that the Scriptures use a number of different metaphors to describe the work of Christ and all of them have something to add to the big picture.

In the next chapter we shall consider the 'nature' of the atonement and spell out the church's teaching on what is called 'penal substitution' which, we shall argue, is the controlling metaphor which brings the various strands of biblical teaching together. In this chapter, as preliminary work, we shall consider several ways in which Jesus is described in the New Testament, which have a bearing on our understanding of his work. In chapter one we already saw that Jesus is Prophet, Priest and King. Here we shall think of Jesus as the last Adam, as Mediator, as the Lamb of God and as great High Priest.

Jesus the last Adam

As we saw in an earlier chapter, 'federal theology' helps us to understand the person of Christ from the perspective of Romans 5 and 1 Corinthians 15. He is the 'second man' or the 'last Adam', who comes to undo the work of Adam and to bring salvation. This understanding of Christ as the Last Adam also flows into an understanding of his work. Christ, through his obedience to God, earns a righteousness for himself through this obedience. God then takes that righteousness of Christ and gives it to those who by faith are 'in Christ'. As part of this 'great exchange' Christ takes our sin and becomes sin for us (2 Corinthians 5:21). He then goes to the cross, in our place, and takes the punishment due to us for our sin. Since we are unable to obtain righteousness through our own perfect obedience to God's law, we receive Christ's righteousness as a free gift, by grace through faith. And since we are unable to pay the penalty for our past sins, Christ does that for us on the cross.

This means that we must focus in on Christ's obedience. To understand this, it is important to know that Christ's obedience to the Father is normally divided into two parts. First, there is his 'active obedience'. This refers to the fact that, throughout his life, Christ perfectly obeyed his Father, did the Father's will and did not sin. Second, there is his 'passive obedience'. This refers to the fact that he permitted himself to be crucified as a sacrificial offering, in the place of sinners. Paul says that he was obedient to death, even death on a cross (Philippians 2:8).

Christ's active obedience

It is clear from the gospels that Christ lived a life of perfect obedience to the Father. No-one could ever point out anything he had done wrong. Indeed, they had to trump up charges in order to accuse him. Jesus on several occasions indicated that his primary task was to offer obedience to the Father. For example, in John 4:34: 'My food,' said Jesus, 'is to do the will of him who sent me and to finish his work.' Then a few chapters later, in John 8:29, Jesus says, 'The one who sent me is with me; he has not left me alone, for I always do what pleases him.'

It is also clear from the New Testament that it is the obedience of Christ which purchases salvation for us. That is stated with particular force in Romans 5:18–19, where Paul writes, 'Consequently, just as the result of one trespass was condemnation for all men, so also the result of one act of righteousness was justification that brings life for all men. For just as through the disobedience of the one man the many were made sinners, so also through the obedience of the one man the many will be made righteous.' In these verses we are told that through the one act of the one man Adam, sin and death came into the world and many died because of this one man's action, since judgement led to condemnation. In parallel to this, we are told that through the one act of the one man Christ, the grace of God abounded for many, leading to the free gift of justification.

What are we to make of the 'one act of righteousness' which brings justification? John Murray's interpretation of 'one act of righteousness' is that it refers to the righteousness of Christ by which we are 'constituted righteous.'[1] He says, 'we must not tone down the formula

---

[1] John Murray, *The Epistle to the Romans: The English Text with Introduction, Exposition and Notes* (London: Marshall, Morgan & Scott, 1960), vol. 1, pp. 201–2.

"constituted righteous" to any lower terms than the gracious judgement on God's part whereby the obedience of Christ is reckoned to our
account and therefore reckoned as ours with all the entail of consequence which righteousness carries with it.[2] The Scriptures teach us a
great deal about the righteousness of Christ which he obtained by his
perfect obedience. Most significantly, we are told in Galatians 2:21 that
there was no other way in which sinners could obtain righteousness:
'if righteousness could be gained through the law, Christ died for
nothing!'

This theme of righteousness forms a central line in Paul's epistles,
especially in the letters to the Romans and the Galatians. Paul believes
that his own people, the Israelites, had tried to obtain righteousness
(get into a right relation with God) by law-keeping and believes that
this was a fundamental mistake, as he spells out in Romans 10:1–4:

> Brothers, my heart's desire and prayer to God for the Israelites is that
> they may be saved. For I can testify about them that they are zealous for
> God, but their zeal is not based on knowledge. Since they did not know
> the righteousness that comes from God and sought to establish their
> own, they did not submit to God's righteousness. Christ is the end of the
> law so that there may be righteousness for everyone who believes.

Paul insists that the only way to be in a right relationship with God is
to obtain the righteousness of Christ, as he says in Philippians 3:7–9:

> But whatever was to my profit I now consider loss for the sake of
> Christ. What is more, I consider everything a loss compared to the sur-
> passing greatness of knowing Christ Jesus my Lord, for whose sake I
> have lost all things. I consider them rubbish, that I may gain Christ and
> be found in him, not having a righteousness of my own that comes
> from the law, but that which is through faith in Christ – the righteous-
> ness that comes from God and is by faith.

Peter says much the same at the beginning of his second letter: 'Simon
Peter, a servant and apostle of Jesus Christ, To those who through the
righteousness of our God and Saviour Jesus Christ have received a
faith as precious as ours . . .'

In Christian theology, the word used to speak of the way in which
Christ takes our sin and we receive his righteousness is 'imputation'.

---

[2] Murray, *Romans*, p. 206.

This has the sense of something being 'reckoned' to another. In the case of salvation, this is a 'double imputation' whereby Christ takes our sin and we receive his righteousness. Both are necessary because if Christ had simply taken our sin and paid the penalty for our sins, then we would have been left precisely in the same position as Adam before the fall, having to obtain a righteousness of our own through obedience to God's law. It is because of Christ's life of obedience that he has obtained a righteousness which he gives to us, through our faith in him. We are then justified before God, not by a righteousness that we have earned but by an 'alien righteousness' (the righteousness of Christ) which comes to us by faith as a free gift of God's grace.

This may sound very complicated and very theological but it is vital to see how practical it is. John Murray was one of the greatest theologians to come out of the Highlands of Scotland. He was a professor of theology at Westminster Theological Seminary in Philadelphia. That seminary was formed by some of the teachers at Princeton Theological Seminary in 1929, when many thought that Princeton was coming under the influence of Liberal Theology. The founder of the seminary was Dr J. Gresham Machen. Machen died in January 1937 and, shortly before he died, he sent a telegram to Professor Murray, who was one of his closest friends. The telegram said, 'I'm so thankful for the active obedience of Christ. No hope without it.'[3]

This doctrine, then, has a very practical application. If Christ had not lived a perfect life, in obedience to the Father, fulfilling every aspect of God's law, then we would have no possibility of justification. That is to say, if Christ had not achieved a righteousness through his active obedience, then that righteousness could not have been imputed to us. When we stand before God we will be clothed in the righteousness of Christ, which has been imputed to us. We have no righteousness of our own; only the righteousness of Christ will save us.

Christ's passive obedience

We now turn to consider Christ's 'passive obedience', which concerns his death on the cross. The critical point here is that Jesus was in complete control of the situation. We must not imagine that his life was

---

[3] Ned B. Stonehouse, *J. Gresham Machen: A Biographical Memoir* (Edinburgh: Banner of Truth, 1977), p. 508.

taken from him by the Jews or the Romans; it was his own willingness to go to the cross and his passive acceptance of his death which constitutes his passive obedience. As Jesus himself said in John 10:14–18:

> I am the good shepherd; I know my sheep and my sheep know me – just as the Father knows me and I know the Father – and I lay down my life for the sheep. I have other sheep that are not of this sheep pen. I must bring them also. They too will listen to my voice, and there shall be one flock and one shepherd. The reason my Father loves me is that I lay down my life – only to take it up again. No-one takes it from me, but I lay it down of my own accord. I have authority to lay it down and authority to take it up again. This command I received from my Father.

Jesus willingly went to the cross and, through this passive obedience, reconciliation took place between God and sinful humanity. By his passive obedience, Jesus brought reconciliation and salvation. The cross achieved what nothing else could achieve: the penalty for sin was paid, another has taken the punishment due to us and we can come into the presence of God without fear because we come in the name of Jesus Christ, clothed in his righteousness.

Jesus the Mediator

The Scriptures teach that there is a gulf fixed between human beings and God because of sin. It is not possible for sinners to come into the presence of a holy God. To remedy this situation, human beings need a mediator. Jesus came to be that mediator and we see this in three ways. First, Jesus is Mediator between God and humanity; second, he is Mediator of a new covenant; and third, he is the only Mediator.

Mediator between God and humanity

The disobedience of our first parents to the clear command of God, as described in Genesis 3, led to them being ejected from the Garden of Eden, symbolic of them being removed from the presence of God. Since that fall of humanity into sin in Genesis 3, there has been a gulf between God and humanity. Human beings, as sinners, could not come into the presence of God. God took some temporary measures to alleviate this situation through the calling of Israel to be the people of God and the institution of the sacrificial and priestly system. By means of the work of the high priest and the various sacrifices, human beings were able to approach near to God. All of this was pointing forward to a time when the temporary measures would come to an end and reconciliation would be accomplished by God himself. This happened when Christ, the Son of God, came as our great High Priest and offered himself as a once-for-all sacrifice for sin. That is why Paul can write in 1 Timothy 2:5, 'For there is one God and one mediator between God and men, the man Christ Jesus'. This description of Christ as a mediator is echoed elsewhere in Scripture. For example, the writer to the Hebrews describes Christ as 'mediator' in 8:6, 9:15 and 12:24.

We ought to pause and ask why this title was used for Christ. We are well used to the word being used in various contexts. When industrial relations break down, a mediator is often called in to help mediate between management and unions. Indeed, the UK government has its own arbitration service, ACAS, for just such occasions. There are also those who work in the area of family mediation, helping to put families back together after they have begun to break down. Mediators are also called in at national and international level. For example, in 1979 Lord Peter Carrington chaired talks at Lancaster House about the future of Rhodesia/Zimbabwe. The key players around the table were Ian Smith, the prime minister of Rhodesia; Joshua Nkomo and Robert Mugabe, leaders of the rebel forces; and Bishop Abel Muzorewa. Carrington acted as a mediator in order to bring peace and an end to the civil war. Another example would be when, in January 1993, Cyrus Vance, the UN special envoy, and David Owen, European Community representative and former British Foreign Secretary, tried to mediate in the Bosnian War in order to bring peace. They sought to be mediators. We could go on to describe many other situations where a mediator helped to bring two or more separated parties together to seek peace and reconciliation.

One of the vital elements in this kind of mediation is that the mediator is independent and has the respect of both sides in the dispute. The best kind of mediator is one who is able to identify with the concerns of both parties. If the mediator is actually representative in some sense of both parties then that, of course, is even better. That is why Christ was the ideal mediator. As we saw in the first part of this book, Jesus is God and he is also a human being. Given that his work as mediator was to reconcile God and human beings, he was uniquely placed to be mediator. Jesus could speak to human beings as God and he could take the place of human beings before God, as substitute and representative.

Mediator of a new covenant

The writer to the Hebrews expresses Christ's role as mediator in the context of what he says about the 'new covenant' instituted by Christ. We see this first in Hebrews 8:6–13:

> But the ministry Jesus has received is as superior to theirs as the covenant of which he is mediator is superior to the old one, and it is founded on better promises. For if there had been nothing wrong with that first covenant, no place would have been sought for another. But God found fault with the people and said: 'The time is coming, declares the Lord, when I will make a new covenant with the house of Israel and with the house of Judah. It will not be like the covenant I made with their forefathers when I took them by the hand to lead them out of Egypt, because they did not remain faithful to my covenant, and I turned away from them, declares the Lord. This is the covenant I will make with the house of Israel after that time, declares the Lord. I will put my laws in their minds and write them on their hearts. I will be their God, and they will be my people. No longer will a man teach his neighbour, or a man his brother, saying, "Know the Lord," because they will all know me, from the least of them to the greatest. For I will forgive their wickedness and will remember their sins no more.' By calling this covenant 'new', he has made the first one obsolete; and what is obsolete and ageing will soon disappear.

This is repeated in Hebrews 9:15, where we are told that 'Christ is the mediator of a new covenant, that those who are called may receive the promised eternal inheritance – now that he has died as a ransom to set them free from the sins committed under the first covenant.' The term 'first covenant' refers to the covenant God made with his people Israel through Moses. In Hebrews 12:24 the writer again speaks about this 'new covenant'. The writer to the Hebrews, throughout his letter, is seeking to establish the superiority of Christ. Hence Christ is superior to the angels, superior to Moses, superior to the high priest and so on. This reference to the 'new covenant' being superior to the 'first covenant' is an extension of that type of argument. It means that the covenant God makes with Christ and those who are in Christ is quite different from what went before. Like the sacrificial system itself, the first covenant was a temporary measure, looking forward to the day when Messiah would come. Now that Christ has come, the new covenant is established through his work as mediator.

The only Mediator

The fact that Jesus Christ is the mediator between God and humanity means that only through him is reconciliation with God to be obtained. As we noted above, 'there is one mediator between God and men, the man Christ Jesus'. This is an expression of the truth that to enter into a right relationship with God, we must come by way of Jesus Christ. That is what Jesus intended us to understand, when he said to his disciples in John 14:6, 'I am the way and the truth and the life. No-one comes to the Father except through me.' Peter expressed the same thought in Acts 4:12, when he said, 'Salvation is found in no-one else, for there is no other name under heaven given to men by which we must be saved.' Jesus Christ was and is the only Mediator between God and ourselves. He speaks to us from God and he speaks to God on our behalf. He stands between us as the one who brings us together in reconciliation.

Jesus the Lamb of God

In Revelation 5 John sees a vision of a scroll. What follows makes it clear that this is a record of the world's destiny. Another way of putting it would be to say that it represents God's plan of redemption. This scroll had seven seals. At the time this was written, there was a custom among the people of this area that what we now call a 'will' or a 'last will and testament' was written in this form, with seven seals. When a person died, the seals were opened, the contents read and the instructions enacted. John's vision suggests that with the breaking of the seals and the opening of the scroll, God's will is made known and then put into effect. There was a problem, however: who was going to break the seals and open the scroll? This is what we find in Revelation 5:1–4:

> Then I saw in the right hand of him who sat on the throne a scroll with writing on both sides and sealed with seven seals. And I saw a mighty angel proclaiming in a loud voice, 'Who is worthy to break the seals and open the scroll?' But no-one in heaven or on earth or under the earth could open the scroll or even look inside it. I wept and wept because no-one was found who was worthy to open the scroll or look inside.

Where could someone be found who was fit to perform this task? In one sense, you see, only God can unlock the secrets of the scroll because only God can make his will known. But then someone was found, as we read in verse 5: 'Then one of the elders said to me, "Do not weep! See, the Lion of the tribe of Judah, the Root of David, has triumphed. He is able to open the scroll and its seven seals."'

Notice that the one who was found to open the scrolls is given two names. He is the 'Lion of the tribe of Judah' and he is the 'Root of David'. Both of these titles are messianic, drawn from the Old Testament, pointing forward to the Messiah who would come. The title 'Lion of the tribe of Judah' comes from Genesis 49:9–10: 'You are a lion's cub, O Judah; you return from the prey, my son. Like a lion he crouches and lies down, like a lioness – who dares to rouse him? The sceptre will not depart from Judah, nor the ruler's staff from between his feet, until he comes to whom it belongs and the obedience of the nations is his.'

The title 'Root of David' comes from Isaiah 11:1–10:

> A shoot will come up from the stump of Jesse; from his roots a Branch will bear fruit. The Spirit of the LORD will rest on him – the Spirit of wisdom and of understanding, the Spirit of counsel and of power, the Spirit of knowledge and of the fear of the LORD – and he will delight in the fear of the LORD. He will not judge by what he sees with his eyes, or decide by what he hears with his ears; but with righteousness he will judge the needy, with justice he will give decisions for the poor of the earth. He will strike the earth with the rod of his mouth; with the breath of his lips he will slay the wicked. Righteousness will be his belt and faithfulness the sash round his waist. The wolf will live with the lamb, the leopard will lie down with the goat, the calf and the lion and the yearling together; and a little child will lead them. The cow will feed with the bear, their young will lie down together, and the lion will eat straw like the ox. The infant will play near the hole of the cobra, and the young child put his hand into the viper's nest. They will neither harm nor destroy on all my holy mountain, for the earth will be full of the knowledge of the LORD as the waters cover the sea. In that day the Root of Jesse will stand as a banner for the peoples; the nations will rally to him, and his place of rest will be glorious.

This means that the Messiah, who was to come, would be a descendant of David but would be greater than David. That is what Jesus explained to the Pharisees in Matthew 22:41–46. Having been asked about the identity of Christ, they replied that he would be 'the son of David'. Jesus then quotes from Psalm 110:1 where David uses the word 'Lord' to refer to the Christ and asks the Pharisees how the Christ can be merely the son of David if David calls him 'Lord'. They have no answer to this and indeed the passage ends by saying that from then on no-one dared to ask him any questions!

With this background we can say that, in Revelation 5:5, John's vision is about Jesus the Messiah. With that background, if we now move on to the next verse of the passage, Revelation 5:6, we find these words: 'Then I saw a Lamb, looking as if it had been slain, standing in the centre of the throne, encircled by the four living creatures and the elders.' After verse 5, we might have been expecting a lion, the Lion of Judah! Instead, we have a lamb. It doesn't seem quite right. If the one who opens the scrolls is the Lion of the tribe of Judah, if he is a descendant of David but greater than David, why is he portrayed as a lamb? In order to understand this, we need to look at a number of passages of Scripture, from both Old and New Testaments.

The first passage, Exodus 12:1–13, concerns the night when God took his people out of Egypt:

> The LORD said to Moses and Aaron in Egypt, 'This month is to be for you the first month, the first month of your year. Tell the whole community of Israel that on the tenth day of this month each man is to take a lamb for his family, one for each household. If any household is too small for a whole lamb, they must share one with their nearest neighbour, having taken into account the number of people there are. You are to determine the amount of lamb needed in accordance with what each person will eat. The animals you choose must be year-old males without defect, and you may take them from the sheep or the goats. Take care of them until the fourteenth day of the month, when all the people of the community of Israel must slaughter them at twilight. Then they are to take some of the blood and put it on the sides and tops of the door-frames of the houses where they eat the lambs. That same night they are to eat the meat roasted over the fire, along with bitter herbs, and bread made without yeast. Do not eat the meat raw or cooked in water, but roast it over the fire – head, legs and inner parts. Do not leave any of it till morning; if some is left till morning, you must burn it. This is how you are to eat it: with your cloak tucked into your belt, your sandals on your feet and your staff in your hand. Eat it in haste; it is the LORD 's Passover. On that same night I will pass through Egypt and strike down every firstborn – both men and animals – and I will

bring judgment on all the gods of Egypt. I am the LORD. The blood will be a sign for you on the houses where you are; and when I see the blood, I will pass over you. No destructive plague will touch you when I strike Egypt.'

John the Baptist

If we now move to the New Testament, we see this passage picked up in the words of John the Baptist in John 1:29: 'The next day John saw Jesus coming towards him and said, "Look, the Lamb of God, who takes away the sin of the world!"'

John the Baptist was already very well known. Crowds were flocking to hear his straightforward and powerful preaching. He denounced the religious establishment and called upon sinners to repent. This was very upsetting to the Jewish leaders, who did not think that they needed to repent. As far as they were concerned, it was only Gentiles who needed to repent. And so they sent a delegation of priests and Levites, to question the Baptist. The issue at stake was his identity. They tried three alternatives: Was he the Christ who was expected? John said 'No.' Was he then Elijah? John answered 'No.' Their final question: Was he the Prophet? This refers to a prophecy in Deuteronomy 18:15–18 which actually referred to the Messiah, as we're told in Acts 3:22 and 7:37, and so once again John answered 'No.'

When they finally ran out of ideas and asked him who he was, John referred them to Isaiah 40:3, which he paraphrased as 'I am the voice of one calling in the desert, "Make straight the way for the Lord."' This, however, did not satisfy the members of the delegation and so they were not yet finished with him. If he was not the Messiah, not Elijah and not the Prophet, then why did he baptize? John answered, 'I baptise with water but among you stands one you do not know. He is the one who comes after me, the thongs of whose sandals I am not worthy to untie.'

Do you see what was happening in this encounter? They wanted John to speak about himself, to reveal his identity. They offered him the opportunity to claim to be someone important, to be the fulfilment of Old Testament prophecy. By contrast, all that John the Baptist wanted to do was to point people to Jesus.

With that background, we can now return to John the Baptist's statement about Jesus: 'Look, the Lamb of God, who takes away the sin of the world!' These words of the Baptist are a summary of his message and they take us to the very heart of the Christian faith. The first thing we must establish, of course, is why John used this strange expression. If we today were to describe someone as a lamb it might be that we considered the person to be gentle or kind but that is not what was in the mind of John the Baptist. As a Jew, he was using language which would immediately have been understood by those who were listening to him. He was making reference to the Passover lamb. In order to explain this we must go back in Jewish history to the time of Joseph.

In the last part of the book of Genesis, we read the story of Joseph and his rise, through various experiences, to a position of leadership within the nation of Egypt. Later, he brought his father Isaac (also called Israel) and his brothers and their families to live with him in Egypt. During the period of years that followed, this family became a nation, known as the Hebrews or Israelites. Later, the pharaoh who had appointed Joseph to a position of leadership died and was replaced by a new king who did not know Joseph and all that he had done for Egypt (Exodus 1:8). Instead of regarding Joseph with gratitude and treating his family with respect, on account of all that Joseph had done to save Egypt from starvation, he and the new leaders in Egypt regarded the Israelites as a danger to their nation and its security. They envisioned a situation where Egypt might be at war and they concluded that the Israelites, who by this time were numerous, might join the enemy and fight against Egypt (Exodus 1:9–10). For this reason, the Israelites lost their freedom and were forced to become the slaves of the Egyptians.

This period of captivity and forced labour led the Hebrews to cry out to God for liberation. God heard, remembered the covenant he had made with Abraham and his descendants and was concerned for the Israelites in Egypt (Exodus 2:23–25). God's answer to their prayer was to send Moses, himself an Israelite although brought up in Pharaoh's house, to lead the people out of Egypt and into a land prepared for them, the 'promised land' (Exodus 3:14–17). God told Moses to go to Pharaoh and tell him to release the Israelites from their slavery and allow them to leave Egypt. Pharaoh refuses this request and indeed repeated requests, as described in Exodus chapters 5 – 10. With each refusal, the Lord sends a plague on Egypt and only ends the plague when Pharaoh promises to allow the Israelites to leave. As soon as each plague passed, however, Pharaoh returned to his intransigent position and the whole cycle was repeated. There were nine plagues in this sequence of events.

Finally, the Lord brought one last plague on Egypt, the plague on the firstborn (Exodus 11). Moses was told to prepare the people for this terrible night when the Lord's judgement would fall upon Egypt. The Lord said that at around midnight he would pass through Egypt and the firstborn in every home would die. In order to distinguish themselves and their homes from those of the Egyptians, each household of the Israelites was to kill a lamb and then spread the blood of the lamb on the doorframes and lintels of their houses. God promised that, as he passed through Egypt in judgement, no death would come to the first-born in the houses which were marked by the blood of the lamb. God duly came in judgement (Exodus 12:29–30) and there was much grief and mourning throughout the land of Egypt. This terrible judgement on the firstborn did not affect any of the homes of the Israelites. In this way, the Israelites sheltered from the judgement of God, under the blood of the lamb.

If we now go back to the words of John the Baptist, we can begin to understand what he meant when he called Jesus the 'Lamb of God who takes away the sin of the world'. Just as the Israelites took shelter under the blood of a lamb, when God passed over Egypt in judgement, so we are to take shelter under the blood of Jesus Christ, the Lamb of God.

This interpretation of the words of John the Baptist is supported elsewhere. Paul says this in 1 Corinthians 5:7: 'Christ, our Passover lamb, has been sacrificed.' There are other passages we could also consider. For example, in Revelation 5, as we have seen, Jesus is described as the Lamb who was slain and it is said that with his blood he 'purchased men for God'.

Now it is possible that someone might ask at this point why we need such shelter. Why do we need to shelter from God's wrath and judgement? The answer is that we are all sinners. The Bible is quite clear on this, that every single human being born on this planet is a sinner cut off from God and is subject to the judgement of God. The only escape from that judgement is to be reconciled to God. If we ask how this is possible, the Bible's answer is simple: 'Believe in the Lord Jesus, and you will be saved' (Acts 16:31).

If we now draw the threads of all this together we can say that, because we are all sinners in need of salvation, God has provided a means of salvation. Just as he provided a way in Egypt for the Israelites to escape from death on that terrible night, so he has pro-vided a way for us to escape the judgement of God on that terrible day when he will judge the world. Just as the blood of a lamb sprin-kled on the doorposts and lintels of the houses was a sign to God that his people were inside, so today we are to shelter under the blood of

Christ, through faith in him. When Jesus died on the cross at Calvary he did so as a sacrificial offering for sin, and God chose to accept the death of Christ in our place.

In order to fully understand the concept of Christ as the Lamb of God, we must also go back to the Old Testament, to a messianic prophecy found in Isaiah 53:7: 'he was led like a lamb to the slaughter, and as a sheep before her shearers is silent, so he did not open his mouth.' If we move to the New Testament, we find this prophecy from Isaiah being picked up in the story of Philip the evangelist in Acts 8:26–35:

> Now an angel of the Lord said to Philip, 'Go south to the road – the desert road – that goes down from Jerusalem to Gaza.' So he started out, and on his way he met an Ethiopian eunuch, an important official in charge of all the treasury of Candace, queen of the Ethiopians. This man had gone to Jerusalem to worship, and on his way home was sitting in his chariot reading the book of Isaiah the prophet. The Spirit told Philip, 'Go to that chariot and stay near it.' Then Philip ran up to the chariot and heard the man reading Isaiah the prophet. 'Do you understand what you are reading?' Philip asked. 'How can I,' he said, 'unless someone explains it to me?' So he invited Philip to come up and sit with him. The eunuch was reading this passage of Scripture: 'He was led like a sheep to the slaughter, and as a lamb before the shearer is silent, so he did not open his mouth. In his humiliation he was deprived of justice. Who can speak of his descendants? For his life was taken from the earth.' The eunuch asked Philip, 'Tell me, please, who is the prophet talking about, himself or someone else?' Then Philip began with that very passage of Scripture and told him the good news about Jesus.

Notice that! Philip takes Isaiah 53 and uses that passage to explain the gospel of Jesus Christ. What does that tell us? Well, it tells us that Isaiah 53 is a messianic passage looking forward to Jesus and that what it says about this Suffering Servant who takes the punishment for others refers to Christ and what he did on the cross. This is supported by something the apostle Peter says in 1 Peter 1:18–19, where we read this: 'For you know that it was not with perishable things such as silver or gold that you were redeemed from the empty way of life handed down to you from your forefathers, but with the precious blood of Christ, a lamb without blemish or defect.' Here we find various scriptural ideas drawn together. The references to Christ as the 'Lamb of God' point to his being sacrificed and to his blood shed for us. If we now go back to Revelation 5:7–14, we see that Christ takes the scroll and opens it. Then he is worshipped:

> He came and took the scroll from the right hand of him who sat on the throne. And when he had taken it, the four living creatures and the twenty-four elders fell down before the Lamb. Each one had a harp and they were holding golden bowls full of incense, which are the prayers of the saints. And they sang a new song: 'You are worthy to take the scroll and to open its seals, because you were slain, and with your blood you purchased men for God from every tribe and language and people and nation. You have made them to be a kingdom and priests to serve our God, and they will reign on the earth.' Then I looked and heard the voice of many angels, numbering thousands upon thousands, and ten thousand times ten thousand. They encircled the throne and the living creatures and the elders. In a loud voice they sang: 'Worthy is the Lamb, who was slain, to receive power and wealth and wisdom and strength and honour and glory and praise!' Then I heard every creature in heaven and on earth and under the earth and on the sea, and all that is in them, singing: 'To him who sits on the throne and to the Lamb be praise and honour and glory and power, for ever and ever!' The four living creatures said, 'Amen', and the elders fell down and worshipped.

The Lamb, we are told, was worthy to open the scroll because he gave his life as a sacrificial offering: 'You are worthy to take the scroll and to open its seals, because you were slain, and with your blood you purchased men for God from every tribe and language and people and nation.' Notice, Christ is to be worshipped because of the atonement. He is the Lamb of God, who was slain so that we might be redeemed.

The blood of the Lamb

This section on Jesus as the Lamb of God would not be complete, however, without making reference to the significance of 'blood' being shed, especially the blood of the Lamb.

In Matthew 26:17–30 we have the passage which describes what has come to be known as the 'last supper', when Jesus ate the Passover meal with his disciples, shortly before his crucifixion. It was during this meal that Jesus used bread and wine to illustrate his death. Ever since that night, Christians have continued this tradition of sharing bread and wine to remind us of the cross. In order to explore something of the meaning of this event (or sacrament), we turn to what Jesus said when he gave them the wine, in verses 28–29. Jesus said, 'This is my blood of the covenant, which is poured out for many for the forgiveness of sins. I tell you, I will not drink of this fruit of the vine from now on until that day when I drink it anew with you in my Father's kingdom.' There are three points to note here. First, the blood of Jesus is 'the blood of the covenant'. Second, the blood of Jesus is poured out for the forgiveness of sins. Third, the blood of Jesus leads to a heavenly celebration.

The blood of Jesus is 'the blood of the covenant'

The first question to be asked is: What did Jesus mean when he spoke about his own blood as the 'blood of the covenant'? To answer that we must go back to the Old Testament, because this expression, 'the blood of the covenant', was first used by Moses:

> When Moses went and told the people all the LORD's words and laws, they responded with one voice, 'Everything the LORD has said we will do.' Moses then wrote down everything the LORD had said. He got up early the next morning and built an altar at the foot of the mountain and set up twelve stone pillars representing the twelve tribes of Israel. Then he sent young Israelite men, and they offered burnt offerings and sacrificed young bulls as fellowship offerings to the LORD. Moses took half of the blood and put it in bowls, and the other half he sprinkled on the altar. Then he took the Book of the Covenant and read it to the people. They responded, 'We will do everything the LORD has said; we will obey.' Moses then took the blood, sprinkled it on the people and said, "This is the blood of the covenant that the LORD has made with you in accordance with all these words' (Exodus 24:3–8).

It is important when we read the New Testament to remember that much of its teaching can only be understood in the light of the Old Testament. That is certainly the case here, with this expression, 'the blood of the covenant'. The disciples who heard Jesus use these words were Jews and they knew their Scriptures. When the disciples heard the words, 'the blood of the covenant', they would immediately have turned their minds to this story in Exodus. They would also have remembered the significance of the blood of the Lamb at the Passover as we find it described in Exodus 12:21–23:

> Then Moses summoned all the elders of Israel and said to them, 'Go at once and select the animals for your families and slaughter the

Passover lamb. Take a bunch of hyssop, dip it into the blood in the basin and put some of the blood on the top and on both sides of the door-frame. Not one of you shall go out of the door of his house until morning. When the LORD goes through the land to strike down the Egyptians, he will see the blood on the top and sides of the door-frame and will pass over that doorway, and he will not permit the destroyer to enter your houses and strike you down.'

In the first passage, the people were cleansed by the blood of the covenant. In the second passage they sheltered under the blood of a lamb. The connection between these stories in Exodus and what Jesus did will be seen most clearly when we come shortly to consider Jesus the great High Priest. Ultimately, we can say that God has provided a way of salvation through the blood of his only Son. God gave Abraham a lamb to sacrifice so that he did not have to sacrifice his son, but God did sacrifice his Son.

The blood of Jesus is poured out for the forgiveness of sins
The second point to notice is what Jesus says about forgiveness. He says, 'This is my blood of the covenant, which is poured out for many for the forgiveness of sins' (Matthew 26:28). This takes us to the very heart of the gospel: Jesus shed his blood so that our sins might be forgiven. If the question is asked regarding the connection between his death on the cross and our forgiveness today, the answer is that we are justified by faith in Jesus Christ. The Shorter Catechism asks, 'What is Justification?' and answers: 'Justification is an act of God's free grace, wherein he pardons all our sins, and accepts us as righteous in his sight, only for the righteousness of Christ imputed to us, and received by faith alone.' Crucial to this, however, is what we find in Hebrews 9:22: 'without the shedding of blood there is no forgiveness.'

In other words, we find forgiveness now, because of what Christ did then. This is the significance of 1 John 1:7, which says, 'the blood of Jesus . . . purifies us from all sin.' That passage of Scripture also tells us that if we say we have no sin we deceive ourselves. That is to say, the first step towards forgiveness is a recognition of our sin. It then goes on to say that if we confess our sins God will forgive us and cleanse us through the blood of Jesus. The other very important point to make is that all of this is by the grace of God, as Paul indicates in Ephesians 2:13: 'But now in Christ Jesus you who once were far away have been brought near through the blood of Christ.' Notice, we do not 'come' near; we are 'brought' near. As the hymn writer says: 'Nothing in my hand I bring, simply to thy cross I cling.'[4] William Still once said that in the Old Testament it was Moses and the people who shed the blood and sprinkled it but in the New Testament it is God, in the person of his Son, who sheds his own blood. We receive the benefits of that by faith.

The blood of Jesus leads to a heavenly celebration
The third point concerns the final part of the passage, where Jesus says, 'I will not drink of this fruit of the vine from now on until that day when I drink it anew with you in my Father's kingdom' (Matthew 26:29). This refers to a significant strand of teaching in the New Testament which speaks about the 'marriage feast' of the Lamb. For example, in Revelation 19:7–9, we read this:

> 'Let us rejoice and be glad and give him glory! For the wedding of the Lamb has come, and his bride has made herself ready. Fine linen, bright and clean, was given her to wear.' (Fine linen stands for the righteous acts of the saints.) Then the angel said to me, 'Write: "Blessed are those who are invited to the wedding supper of the Lamb!"' And he added, 'These are the true words of God.'

Jesus once told a parable about a marriage feast in Matthew 22:1–14, the main point being that many are invited but few are chosen. Jesus was teaching that this great wedding feast lies ahead of us but that we must be properly dressed in order to attend. The man who was not dressed in the proper wedding garments was thrown out. This means that we must be clothed in the righteousness of Christ. There will come a day, then, when those who have been redeemed by the blood of Christ will gather in heaven to share in the marriage feast of the Lamb. When Jesus shared the bread and wine with his disciples, he was looking forward to the cross. He was also looking even further forward to that day when everything will be completed and the great wedding feast of the Lamb takes place in heaven. When we share together in the bread and wine, we do so with the anticipation of that great day when we shall meet together with the risen Lord in glory and share in that great feast. All of this is summed up in the words of an old redemption hymn:

---

[4] Augustus M. Toplady, 'Rock of Ages', 1776.

Have you been to Jesus for the cleansing power?
Are you washed in the blood of the Lamb?
Are you fully trusting in His grace this hour?
Are you washed in the blood of the Lamb?

Are you washed in the blood,
In the soul-cleansing blood of the Lamb?
Are your garments spotless? Are they white as snow?
Are you washed in the blood of the Lamb?

Are you walking daily by the Savior's side?
Are you washed in the blood of the Lamb?
Do you rest each moment in the Crucified?
Are you washed in the blood of the Lamb?

When the Bridegroom cometh will your robes be white?
Are you washed in the blood of the Lamb?
Will your soul be ready for the mansions bright
And be washed in the blood of the Lamb?

Lay aside the garments that are stained with sin
And be washed in the blood of the Lamb;
There's a fountain flowing for the soul unclean,
O be washed in the blood of the Lamb![5]

Jesus the great High Priest

As we read on in the New Testament we discover that Christ is not simply the sacrificial Lamb, but also the High Priest who offers the Lamb as a sacrifice to God. In other words, the one who was slain as a sacrifice is also the one who offers the sacrifice.

In the Old Testament, God laid down a form of worship and service which was based on blood sacrifices. At the heart of this system was the most important day in the Jewish calendar, the Day of Atonement. In Leviticus 16, we read about the institution of the Day of Atonement. Aaron, the brother of Moses, was the high priest of Israel and it was his function, along with all the other priests, to offer sacrifices to God. The number and the types of sacrifices were laid

---

[5] Elisha A. Hoffman, 1878.

down by God. Aaron, however, had one duty which was peculiar to himself as high priest and which could not be performed by any of the other priests. On the Day of Atonement, once each year, on the tenth day of the seventh month, Aaron was to enter into the Most Holy Place (sometimes called the 'Holy of Holies'). This was the inner sanctuary of the Tent of Meeting (and later of the Temple). No-one else was ever allowed into this inner sanctum and even the high priest only went in on this one important day in the year.

On the Day of Atonement, the high priest offered sacrifices, to make atonement for the whole people of God. He first of all made atonement for the Tent of Meeting itself, including the Most Holy Place. Then he offered a sacrifice for his own sins and for the sins of the people of Israel. This ritual was to be repeated every year without fail. As we read in Leviticus 16:34, 'This is to be a lasting ordinance for you: Atonement is to be made once a year for all the sins of the Israelites.' The high priest was not elected; rather he was chosen and appointed by God from among the people. It was also necessary that the high priest be morally pure and consecrated to the service of God (Leviticus 21:6; Psalm 106:16).

Since in the Old Testament there was this high priest who offered sacrifices to God on behalf of the people (particularly that great sacrifice on the Day of Atonement), the Jews knew that God had provided a way of dealing with their sins. This meant that, in answer to the question 'How can sinners come into the presence of a holy God?' the Jews could answer, 'They can come because the high priest has gone to God on their behalf and has made atonement. Their sins have been passed over and God will not hold these sins against them.'

When we turn to the New Testament, however, Hebrews 9 tells us that Jesus is our High Priest in a way that no other could ever have been. Jesus comes as the mediator of a new and better covenant and he is a new and better High Priest. The high priest of the Jews offered the same sacrifices year after year but Jesus, with one sacrifice, put an end to all that. The high priest in the Old Testament entered into the Most Holy Place to offer the sacrifice of atonement, but Jesus entered into heaven itself. The blood of goats and calves did not really cleanse men and women from sin – they only made them 'ceremonially' clean – but the blood of Christ actually cleanses from sin, once and for all. The high priest in the Old Testament had to offer sacrifices for his own sins as well as those of the people, but Jesus was without sin.

What we can see, then, by comparing Leviticus 16 and Hebrews 9, is that Calvary had a much deeper meaning than we are sometimes given to imagine. Everything we read in the Old Testament about sacrifices and priests and so on was brought to a conclusion in the cross. The plan of God for the salvation of his people did not begin when Jesus was born. Rather the whole Bible stands together and we can see the fulfilment in Christ of all the temporary measures (the entire sacrificial system) of the Old Testament.

If we now go back to an incident in the gospels it will help us to understand the full significance of the high priesthood of Jesus. In Matthew 27:50–51 we are told that at the very moment Jesus died, the curtain in the Temple was torn in two. Now that curtain was the curtain between the sanctuary and the Most Holy Place. That is to say, it was the curtain which the high priest passed through, going into the Most Holy Place on the Day of Atonement each year. Suddenly, everyone could see into the Most Holy Place. Suddenly the barrier between the Most Holy Place and the remainder of the temple had been taken away. Why did this happen? Well, it was a sign from God that the Jewish high priest was not needed any more. Jesus had fulfilled with one sacrifice everything which was previously done by the high priest and this had been accepted by God on behalf of his people. Anyone can now come into the nearer presence of God, not just one man on one day in the year. More important still, when we do come into the nearer presence of God, we don't come bearing a blood sacrifice. The debt for sin has already been fully paid.

The continuing work of Christ in intercession

Put at its simplest, we now have free and unrestricted access into the presence of God. Jesus has made a new and living way for us to come into the presence of God; all the barriers of the old dispensation have gone. Even this, however, is not the end of the story. When the Bible tells us that Jesus is our great High Priest and that he is the only mediator between God and man (1 Timothy 2:5–6), it is not only speaking about what he did in the past for us on Calvary but what he continues to do for us now. The Bible assures us that Jesus, even now, is praying for us and making intercession for us before the throne of God.

To understand this continuing ministry of Christ in intercession, we need to consider the nature of Christ's intercession, looking at both its earthly and heavenly dimensions.

The teaching of the New Testament is that when Christ had finished the work he was given to do on this earth, he ascended into heaven. He is now seated at the right hand of God and in that place his ministry continues, through his intercession on behalf of believers. We must remember, of course, that his intercession began while he was on this earth.

The earthly intercession of Christ

There are various examples of the prayers of Jesus during his earthly ministry. For example, at the grave of Lazarus (John 11:38–42) and also when he foretold Peter's denial (Luke 22:31–34). The most striking passage, of course, is John 17, often called the 'high priestly prayer' of Jesus, particularly verses 6–10:

> I have revealed you to those whom you gave me out of the world. They were yours; you gave them to me and they have obeyed your word. Now they know that everything you have given me comes from you. For I gave them the words you gave me and they accepted them. They knew with certainty that I came from you, and they believed that you sent me. I pray for them. I am not praying for the world, but for those you have given me, for they are yours. All I have is yours, and all you have is mine. And glory has come to me through them.

Notice also verses 20–21: 'My prayer is not for them alone. I pray also for those who will believe in me through their message, that all of them may be one, Father, just as you are in me and I am in you. May they also be in us so that the world may believe that you have sent me.'

The key points here are that Jesus is only praying for believers and those who would one day become believers. This is quite important because, as our priest, Jesus prays for those for whom he died. Both parts of his priestly ministry are focussed on God's chosen people.

One important question, of course, is this: What is Jesus praying for? Derek Thomas says that we should learn from this prayer of Jesus in John 17 and recognize that Jesus is praying for the same things now in heaven as he was when he was on earth. Dr Thomas identifies five things for which Jesus prays:

1. He prays that his disciples might be protected;
2. He prays that we might have joy;
3. He prays for the church's unity;

4. He wills that we may be with him;

5. He wants them to see his glory.[6]

The heavenly intercession of Christ

With those few words about the earthly intercession of Jesus, we come to our main theme, the intercession of the ascended Lord. We should note two general points as we begin to open up this theme. First, like the atonement itself, the intercessory ministry of Christ comes from the Father's love. In other words, God does not have to be persuaded to love us by Christ dying for us and praying for us. It was because God loved the world so much that he sent his Son in the first place. Similarly, when Christ prays for us he is not trying to persuade an unwilling and unloving God to take pity on us. Rather, the ministry of intercession was given to him by the Father, because of the love of the Father. John Murray put it like this: 'As in the propitiation itself, there is no place for the notion that the Father is won over to clemency and grace by inducements which the Son brings to bear upon him. Just as the propitiation is the provision of the Father's love, so must we say that the intercession is also.'[7]

Second, we must not imagine that, because Christ continues to intercede for us, somehow the atonement was incomplete. Rather we must recognize that, on the cross, Christ paid the penalty for sins once and for all. That sacrifice does not need to be repeated. All that is necessary for our salvation has been accomplished. The purpose of the continuing intercession of Christ is to plead our case before the Father *on the basis* of what he has accomplished. The intercession does not add to the atonement. There are several passages in the New Testament which speak of this, including Romans 8:31–34:

> What, then, shall we say in response to this? If God is for us, who can be against us? He who did not spare his own Son, but gave him up for us all – how will he not also, along with him, graciously give us all things? Who will bring any charge against those whom God has chosen? It is God who justifies. Who is he that condemns? Christ Jesus, who died – more than that, who was raised to life – is at the right hand of God and is also interceding for us.

---

[6] Derek Thomas, *Taken Up to Heaven: The Ascension of Christ* (Darlington: Evangelical Press, 1996), pp. 124–6.

[7] Murray, *Collected Writings*, vol. 1, p. 57.

This passage addresses the question of certainty and assurance. Having become a Christian, how can I be sure that I will remain a Christian? Paul makes it clear that those who are in Christ will persevere to the end and he gives various reasons. In these verses, he makes the point that there is no condemnation for those that are in Christ Jesus and then he says that Christ is at the right hand of God interceding for us. In this context, the intercession of Christ is portrayed as ensuring our safe arrival in heaven. That is to say, it concerns the perseverance of the saints and the assurance of salvation. It gives us hope.

Another helpful reference is Hebrews 7:25, where we read these words about Jesus: 'Therefore he is able to save completely those who come to God through him, because he always lives to intercede for them.' A couple of chapters further on, in Hebrews 9:24, we are told that Christ 'entered heaven itself, now to appear for us in God's presence.' Notice that 'for us'. Do you see what is being said here? Christ 'is able to save completely those who come to God through him, because he always lives to intercede for them.' What does this mean? It means that the intercession of Christ is part of the overall work which Christ does to ensure our salvation. We will be saved 'completely' because he is always there to intercede for us. In this case, the reference is to Christ as our great High Priest who, having offered a sacrifice on our behalf, continues to pray for us. This is the idea behind one verse of a well-known hymn:

Before the throne of God above
I have a strong and perfect plea:
A great High Priest whose Name is Love
Who ever lives and pleads for me.[8]

The final New Testament reference we need to consider is in 1 John 2:1–2: 'My dear children, I write this to you so that you will not sin. But if anybody does sin, we have one who speaks to the Father in our defence – Jesus Christ, the Righteous One. He is the atoning sacrifice for our sins, and not only for ours but also for the sins of the whole world.' This picture of intercession is taken from the imagery of the courtroom. John tells us that we should not sin but, if we do, there is an advocate who speaks a word of defence or mitigation to God on our behalf. In this case the intercession concerns our sins. Every time we sin we can come to the Father through our advocate, our Mediator. Christ intercedes on our behalf.

---

[8] Charitie I. Bancroft, 1863.

All of these passages, taken together, paint a wonderful picture of Christ's intercession. We should also be aware, however, that as well as this clear teaching from the New Testament, there is a passage we should consider from the Old Testament. In the book of Job we often find Job expressing insights which we might expect to find only in the New Testament. For example, he says, 'I know that my Redeemer lives' (Job 19:25). On this matter of having an intercessor in heaven, he also has something to say. In Job 16:16–22 we read this:

> My face is red with weeping, deep shadows ring my eyes; yet my hands have been free of violence and my prayer is pure. O earth, do not cover my blood; may my cry never be laid to rest! Even now my witness is in heaven; my advocate is on high. My intercessor is my friend as my eyes pour out tears to God; on behalf of a man he pleads with God as a man pleads for his friend. Only a few years will pass before I go on the journey of no return.

In these passages we see the nature of Christ's intercession. The Christian life begins when, through faith in Jesus Christ and in his completed work, we come to a knowledge of God and enter into a relationship with God. When this happens, sanctification begins and goes on until we die. This whole process is supported by all that Christ has done (incarnation, life, death, resurrection and ascension) and all that he continues to do (intercession). For this reason, it can never be lost and will last through all eternity.

In all of this, we must remember that the intercession of Christ springs from the love of God, as expressed in the second verse of the hymn 'O the Deep, Deep Love of Jesus':

> O the deep, deep love of Jesus,
> Spread His praise from shore to shore!
> How He loveth, ever loveth,
> Changeth never, nevermore!
>
> How He watches o'er His loved ones,
> Died to call them all His own;
> How for them He intercedeth,
> Watcheth o'er them from the throne![9]

---

[9] S. Trevor Francis, 1875.

We are all in need of the intercession of Christ. It is part of his work and is the completion of all that he did during his earthly ministry.

In my ministry I have often been encouraged by the prayers of friends, especially in times of difficulty. I value this prayer support very much and am encouraged to think of how the Lord will use these prayers of my family and friends. Perhaps you too have been encouraged, strengthened and helped by the prayers of family and friends. Imagine, then, how we ought to feel about the fact that Christ is praying for us! What a great privilege to be those for whom the Son of God prays!

A well-known paraphrase of Hebrews 4 puts the whole matter very well:

> Where high the heavenly temple stands,
> The house of God not made with hands,
> A great High Priest our nature wears,
> The Guardian of mankind appears.
>
> He who for men their surety stood,
> And poured on earth his precious blood,
> Pursues in heaven his mighty plan,
> The Saviour and the Friend of man.
>
> With boldness, therefore, at the throne,
> Let us make all our sorrows known;
> And ask the aids of heavenly power,
> To help us in the evil hour.[10]

Conclusion

When most people think about the cross, all they see is a good man wrongly put to death, by wicked religious leaders, in partnership with a corrupt regime. As Christians, we must look deeper. A great transaction was taking place on that cross. Something was happening which has life-saving and life-changing potential. Jesus the last Adam came to undo what Adam did and to rescue the human race. He came as the Mediator between God and human beings and in this capacity brought reconciliation. Jesus is also the Lamb of God, who takes away

[10] Michael Bruce, 1764.

the sins of the world. Paradoxically, he is also our great High Priest. He offers one sacrifice, on the cross at Calvary, and that brings an end to all sacrifices. The sacrifice he offers is himself and so we have this strange coming together of two key themes: the priest offers a lamb but Christ is both the Priest and the Lamb! He is the one who offers the sacrifice and he is the sacrifice itself. Having done all of this, he continues his ministry as High Priest through his intercession for us before the throne of God.

8

The Nature of the Atonement

Introduction

In our studies in the person and work of Christ, we come now to consider the nature of the atonement. The word 'atonement' means to reconcile or to bring together those who have previously been estranged. In Christian theology, it refers to the action of Christ in bringing reconciliation between God and sinners. In the Authorised Version of the Bible, 'atonement' is used in Romans 5:10–11: 'For if, when we were enemies, we were reconciled to God by the death of his Son, much more, being reconciled, we shall be saved by his life. And not only so, but we also joy in God through our Lord Jesus Christ, by whom we have now received the atonement.' The atonement, then, is the work which Christ has done in order to reconcile us to God.[1]

In the last chapter we looked at some of the core biblical teaching concerning the work of Christ. In the history of the church, however, this teaching has been interpreted in various ways and different 'theories of atonement' have been developed to provide an overview of the meaning and significance of the atonement. From the time of the Reformation, however, in Reformed and evangelical churches, the controlling idea has been the penal substitutionary view of the atonement. Many today reject this teaching on penal substitution. Some theologians will even admit that penal substitution is taught in Scripture but they go on to say that we are not bound by that. Even some evangelicals challenge this teaching. They either say that the Bible does not teach penal substitution, or they say that penal substitution is only one

---

[1] For a biblical and theological explanation of the doctrine of the atonement, see John Murray, *Redemption Accomplished and Applied* (Grand Rapids, MI: Eerdmans, 1955); Leon Morris, *The Apostolic Preaching of the Cross* (Leicester: IVP, 1965); Leon Morris, *The Atonement: Its Meaning and Significance* (Leicester: IVP, 1983); Paul Wells, *Cross Words: The Biblical Doctrine of the Atonement* (Fearn: CFP, 2006).

model among many and therefore ought not to be the controlling interpretive theme in our theology of atonement. In this chapter we are
going to show from Scripture why we believe that this penal substitutionary view encapsulates most fully the breadth of biblical teaching on
the atonement. Then, in the next chapter, we are going to provide a biblical and theological defence of this view, not least by comparing and
contrasting it with other atonement theories.

Biblical metaphors

It is important, as we begin, to say a word about biblical metaphors in
respect of the atonement. The *Oxford English Dictionary* defines a
metaphor in this way: 'A figure of speech in which a name or descrip-
tive word or phrase is transferred to an object or action different from,
but analogous to, that to which it is literally applicable.' Jesus used
metaphors to describe himself on various occasions; for example, 'I
am the bread of life' (John 6:48) and 'I am the gate' (John 10:9).

A range of different metaphors is used in Scripture to help us
understand the atonement. There are judicial or forensic metaphors,
where the language of the courtroom is used to describe the transaction which has taken place between the Father and the Son on our
behalf (Romans 3:25–26). There are also metaphors of sacrifice, relating what Jesus did on the cross to the sacrifices offered in the Temple
in the Old Covenant (1 Corinthians 5:7). We also find metaphors of
redemption, where a ransom price is paid by Christ to set sinners free
(Mark 10:45). When we take all of these metaphors together, we get a
fuller and deeper picture of the nature of the atonement.

More recently, however, there have been those who have used the
multiplicity of metaphors as an excuse for not taking any one of them
too seriously. The writers who argue in this way (and we shall refer to
some of them in the next chapter) do not want to be bound by
metaphors, particularly those which emphasize sacrificial or forensic
language. Indeed, some of them argue that we are not limited simply
by the metaphors we already have in Scripture but should feel free to
create our own metaphors which might more easily connect with our
modern society. Those who argue in this way have most commonly
been trying to find ways of dispensing with the forensic and sacrificial metaphors because they do not believe what these metaphors
convey. In contradistinction to these views, we affirm that the range
of metaphors, when taken together, do not contradict or undermine

each other but rather they provide a rich and full picture of what Christ has done. Indeed, they strengthen the case for a penal and substitutionary view of the atonement.[2]

Penal substitution

The important question facing any atonement theory concerns how the death of one man, over 2,000 years ago, can bring salvation to human beings. To explain this, Christian theologians have used two words, 'penalty' and 'substitution', giving the expression 'penal substitution'.[3] As we consider the nature of the atonement, we shall focus in on these two key elements of any biblical understanding of atonement, namely, 'penalty' and 'substitution'. We shall then consider Isaiah 53 and Romans 3, two passages which teach these key elements.

Penalty

The first idea is 'penalty'. This means that there was a penalty to be paid for sin and Jesus came and paid that penalty himself on the cross. Paul deals with this in his letter to the Romans. In 3:23 he notes that 'all have sinned and fall short of the glory of God'. Then in 6:23 he says that 'the wages of sin is death, but the gift of God is eternal life in Christ Jesus our Lord.' The implication here is that human beings are sinners and that this sin attracts a penalty, the penalty being death. This penalty of death is contrasted with the free gift of eternal life. In the flow of the teaching in the letter to the Romans, we might summarize it in this way: all human beings are sinners and because of their sinful condition they are subject to the judgement of God. The judgement which God pronounces on sin is that it must be punished by death. Nevertheless, out of his mercy, love and wisdom, God sends his own Son to take this penalty.

When Christ pays this penalty (on the cross), the alienation between God and sinners is repaired and those who are 'in Christ' are reconciled to God. In Colossians 1:21–22 Paul shows us the harsh,

---

[2] See Henri Blocher, 'Biblical Metaphors and the Doctrine of Atonement', *JETS* 47:4 (2004): pp. 629–45.

[3] The best short explanation of this doctrine is J.I. Packer's article 'What Did the Cross Achieve? The Logic of Penal Substitution', *TynBul* 25 (1974): pp. 3–45.

objective truth about the death of Christ: 'Once you were alienated from God and were enemies in your minds because of your evil behaviour. But now he has reconciled you by Christ's physical body through death to present you holy in his sight, without blemish and free from accusation.'

Substitution

The second idea is 'substitution'. At its very simplest, Paul expresses it in this way, in Romans 5:8: 'God demonstrates his own love for us in this: While we were still sinners, Christ died for us.' We also see this theme of substitution in the inadvertent words of the high priest Caiaphas, in John 11:50–52:

> 'You do not realise that it is better for you that one man die for the people than that the whole nation perish.' He did not say this on his own, but as high priest that year he prophesied that Jesus would die for the Jewish nation, and not only for that nation but also for the scattered children of God, to bring them together and make them one.

It is there too in the great 'resurrection chapter', in 1 Corinthians 15:3: 'Christ died for our sins according to the Scriptures'.

There are numerous references which speak in the same general way. For example, it is said of Christ, in Titus 2:14, that he 'gave himself for us to redeem us from all wickedness and to purify for himself a people that are his very own, eager to do what is good.' It was not only Paul who used this imagery of substitution; we find it also in Peter. For Peter, the substitution involved Christ taking our sin and bearing that sin to the cross, as we read in 1 Peter 2:24: 'He himself bore our sins in his body on the tree, so that we might die to sins and live for righteousness; by his wounds you have been healed.' In the next chapter, Peter sums up substitutionary language with a wonderful description of what Christ has done for us. In 1 Peter 3:18 he says, 'For Christ died for sins once for all, the righteous for the unrighteous, to bring you to God.'

The substitutionary death of Christ is also found in 2 Corinthians 5:21: 'God made him who had no sin to be sin for us, so that in him we might become the righteousness of God.' It is here that the substitution is seen as the heart of the doctrine of justification by faith. This is a key text which deserves close examination, not least because it opens up for us an understanding of the meaning of the gospel itself.

As we read the text, certain things are immediately obvious. First, the context of verses 17–20 make it clear that this verse is speaking about Jesus Christ. He is the one who was without sin but has become sin. Second, God did this 'for us'. That is to say, Christ became sin as part of God's plan for our salvation. It is, therefore, because Christ became sin that we can become 'the righteousness of God.'

Those who are not familiar with this verse of Scripture might find the concept of Christ 'becoming sin' a difficult notion to grasp. The great Reformer John Calvin, in his commentary on this passage, makes the point even more forcefully when he says that Christ became a sinner.[4] Now Calvin was very careful to emphasize that Christ never sinned and that there was no moral fault in his life. He lived from beginning to end a perfect life without any disobedience to God or any breach of God's law. Rather, Christ is 'reckoned' by God to be a sinner because he voluntarily took the place of sinners. We might put it like this: On the cross at Calvary Jesus Christ was regarded by God as a guilty sinner and was punished by God for the sins of others. He was not a sinner because he sinned but because he voluntarily took the place of sinners.

There is an illustration which might help us understand this fact of Christ taking our place. This illustration is offered tentatively, since no human illustration can fully express the wonder and mystery of the gospel, but it might help. Imagine a man who is a serious drinker and gambler. He lives a life devoted to these pursuits and gradually falls into debt. As he gambles more and more to try and recover his money, so the debt increases, and as he realizes the impossible nature of his situation so he drinks more and more. All the time his debts are building up. Then suddenly, the man dies. The man has a son, who is his next of kin. Now the son has never been a gambler or a drinker but because he is the next of kin and because he loved his father dearly, he does not disown his father but rather he freely and voluntarily takes on the debts which his father had accumulated and promises to pay them himself. Those to whom the father owed money now come to the son and demand the money from him. The son cannot say that he has never been a drinker or a gambler, because he has freely chosen to make himself liable for his father's debts. He himself is without fault in the matter of drinking and gambling, but he is now the one responsible for the debts.

---

[4] John Calvin, *The Second Epistle of Paul the Apostle to the Corinthians*, in Calvin's *Commentaries* (ed. T.F. Torrance and D.W. Torrance; Edinburgh: Oliver & Boyd, 1964), p. 81.

In the same way, Jesus Christ never sinned, but he freely and voluntarily chose to take the place of sinners and receive from God the punishment which was due to them. For this to happen he had to become sin. This is similar to what Paul says in Galatians 3:13 when he says that Christ became 'a curse' for us. You see, in order that we might be saved two things were necessary. First, it was necessary that someone should take the punishment for our sin and second, it was necessary that the one who took the punishment for our sin should himself be sinless. This latter point is made clear in a number of places in Scripture, including Hebrews 4:15; 1 Peter 2:22; and 1 John 3:5.

That, then, is the sense in which Christ 'became sin'. He became sin because God 'reckoned' or 'accounted' him to be sin, in order that he might die in the place of sinners. That leads naturally to the other half of the verse. Christ became sin in order that believers might become the righteousness of God. To understand this, we must first examine the meaning of the word 'righteousness' as it is being used in this verse of Scripture. The word 'righteousness' is used in two different ways in the New Testament. On the one hand, it is used in a moral sense to refer to the holiness and morality and goodness which the Holy Spirit produces in the life of a believer through the process of sanctification. On the other hand, however, it is used in a forensic or legal sense, to describe our relation to God's law. In our text, the word 'righteousness' is used in the second sense. As Professor Charles Hodge put it, 'It expresses our relation to the law, not our inward moral state.'[5]

Having established the meaning of the word 'righteousness', we are now in a position to ask the question, 'In what sense have sinners become righteous?' The answer is that sinners have become righteous in the sense that they have been *declared* by God to be righteous. In other words, as Christians we are not righteous in the sense that we are completely holy and do not sin; rather we are righteous in the sense that God has declared us to be righteous in relation to his law. This is well expressed in the words of John Calvin:

> We may now return to the contrast drawn in this verse between righteousness and sin. How can we become righteous before God? In the same way as Christ became a sinner. For he took, as it were, our person, that he might be the offender in our name and thus might be reckoned

[5] Charles Hodge, *A Commentary on 1 and 2 Corinthians* (Edinburgh: Banner of Truth, 1978), p. 526.

a sinner, not because of his own offences but because of those of others, since he himself was pure and free from every fault and bore the penalty that was our due and not his own. Now in the same way we are righteous in him, not because we have satisfied God's judgement by our own works, but because we are judged in relation to Christ's righteousness which we have put on by faith, that it may become our own.[6]

The point is an important one. Christ became a sinner not because he sinned but because *he took our sin*. In the same way we become righteous, not because we have stopped sinning but because *we have received his righteousness*. This has been called 'the great exchange'. Jesus Christ takes our sin and in exchange we receive his righteousness. If we further ask the means by which we receive this righteousness, the answer is that we receive his righteousness by faith in Christ. This is explained very clearly in the early chapters of Paul's letter to the Romans where Paul explains how we can be 'right' with God. Having demonstrated that no human being can be right with God through keeping the law (either the Law given through Moses to the Jews, or the law known to the Gentiles), Paul demonstrates that the only way to be right with God is by faith.

Here is the heart of the doctrine of justification by faith. We are not justified before God because we have a righteousness of our own but because we have received as a free gift the righteousness of Christ. If we properly understand this great exchange, then we can see the implications for the forgiveness of sins. When they stand before God on the Day of Judgement, Christians can be absolutely sure of their salvation because it does not depend upon human attempts at self-justification or even acts of righteousness but rather upon the righteousness of Christ which has been given to them as a free gift.

Although there are other metaphors of atonement, this metaphor of penal substitution is the controlling metaphor, which enables us to understand all the others within a context, as we shall see now, in two significant biblical passages.

Isaiah 53

We have noted that 'penalty' and 'substitution' are at the heart of what we understand by atonement. If we turn now to Isaiah 53, we find these themes clearly stated, not least in verses 4–7 of that chapter:

---

[6] Calvin, *Second Epistle of Paul to the Corinthians* (ed. Torrance and Torrance), pp. 81–2.

> Surely he took up our infirmities and carried our sorrows, yet we considered him stricken by God, smitten by him, and afflicted. But he was pierced for our transgressions, he was crushed for our iniquities; the punishment that brought us peace was upon him, and by his wounds we are healed. We all, like sheep, have gone astray, each of us has turned to his own way; and the LORD has laid on him the iniquity of us all. He was oppressed and afflicted, yet he did not open his mouth; he was led like a lamb to the slaughter, and as a sheep before her shearers is silent, so he did not open his mouth.

Notice what is being said here. First in verse 4: 'Surely he took up our infirmities and carried our sorrows.' Then in verse 5: 'But he was pierced for our transgressions, he was crushed for our iniquities; the punishment that brought us peace was upon him, and by his wounds we are healed.' Then verse 6: 'We all, like sheep, have gone astray, each of us has turned to his own way; and the LORD has laid on him the iniquity of us all.' Finally, in verse 7, the Suffering Servant is described as being 'led like a lamb to the slaughter'. In these very clear statements, this famous chapter of Scripture takes us to the heart of the meaning of the atonement. This is one of the famous 'Servant Songs' of Isaiah, which point forward prophetically to the coming of the Messiah. On the basis of Acts 8:26–35, as we saw in the last chapter, it has long been the conviction of Reformed and evangelical biblical scholars (and millions of Christians) that this passage was fulfilled in the life and death of Jesus Christ. We are going to use this chapter as the starting point from which we will go forward into the New Testament, where we will see how some of these prophecies were fulfilled. In particular, we shall note four themes here in Isaiah 53:

1. The Suffering Servant was born in order to die.
2. The Suffering Servant takes upon himself the sins of others.
3. The Suffering Servant as a substitute takes the punishment for others.
4. The Suffering Servant makes intercession for others.

The Suffering Servant was born in order to die
Isaiah 53 was written over 700 years before Jesus was born and yet it clearly and accurately predicts what was going to happen to Jesus of Nazareth. This means that the death of his Son was in the mind and plan of God long before the events leading up to Calvary took place.

If we now move forward into the New Testament, we find some helpful teaching from the mouth of Jesus himself. In John 12:27, while prophesying about his own death, Jesus says this: 'Now my heart is troubled, and what shall I say? "Father save me from this hour"? No, it was for this very reason I came to this hour.' In other words, Jesus tells us that his reason for coming to earth was to die! There are some who believe that the death of such a man was a tragedy, but no, it was planned from the very beginning. On a number of occasions Jesus told his disciples exactly what was going to happen. In John 10:17–18, for example, he is recorded as saying, 'The reason my Father loves me is that I lay down my life – only to take it up again. No-one takes it from me, but I lay it down of my own accord.' The same teaching is found in Acts 2:22,23: 'Men of Israel, listen to this: Jesus of Nazareth was a man accredited by God to you by miracles, wonders and signs, which God did among you through him, as you yourselves know. This man was handed over to you by God's set purpose and fore-knowledge; and you, with the help of wicked men, put him to death by nailing him to the cross.'

If we take the Scriptures seriously, then, we will see that the death of Jesus was no mistake but was in the plan of God from the beginning. Indeed we must go as far as Jesus did and say that the very purpose of the incarnation was the crucifixion. Jesus was born in order to die.

The Suffering Servant takes upon himself the sins of others
This teaching is to be found in Isaiah 53:4, where we read, 'Surely he took up our infirmities and carried our sorrows.' Again, in verse 6, we read, 'We all, like sheep, have gone astray, each of us has turned to his own way; and the Lord has laid on him the iniquity of us all.'

This teaching is also to be found as we go forward into the New Testament. In John 1:29 John the Baptist says, 'Look, the Lamb of God, who takes away the sin of the world!' As we saw in a previous chapter, these words of the Baptist are a summary of his message and they take us to the very heart of the Christian faith. John meant that, just as the Israelites in Egypt took shelter under the blood of a lamb and so escaped when the angel of death passed over, so we are to take shelter under the blood of Jesus Christ to escape from God's wrath and judgement today.

The Suffering Servant, as a substitute, takes the punishment for others
This teaching is to be found in Isaiah 53:5, which reads, 'But he was pierced for our transgressions, he was crushed for our iniquities; the punishment that brought us peace was upon him, and by his wounds we are healed.' We also find it in Isaiah 53:7 where the Suffering Servant is described as being 'led like a lamb to the slaughter'.

If we now move to the New Testament and ask the question, 'What did the death of Christ achieve?' we find that Jesus himself gives us the answer in those famous words from the Last Supper: 'This is my blood of the covenant, which is poured out for many for the forgiveness of sins' (Matthew 26:28). This is the key to the whole subject, the forgiveness of sins, and yet it immediately raises another question, namely, how can the death of one man two thousand years ago bring forgiveness of sins to us today? There are many ways of answering that question but the most basic answer is very simple: God punished Jesus instead of punishing us. Here is the heart of the meaning of the penal substitutionary theory of the atonement.

The Suffering Servant makes intercession for others
Isaiah 53:12 says, 'For he bore the sin of many and made intercession for the transgressors.' As we saw in the last chapter, this teaching from Isaiah is reflected in what the New Testament writers say about the heavenly intercession of Christ.

Romans 3:21–26

Having seen this emphasis on penal, substitutionary atonement prophetically in Isaiah, it is no surprise to find that this is also the controlling motif in the New Testament. The classic passage is Romans 3:21–26:

> But now a righteousness from God, apart from law, has been made known, to which the Law and the Prophets testify. This righteousness from God comes through faith in Jesus Christ to all who believe. There is no difference, for all have sinned and fall short of the glory of God, and are justified freely by his grace through the redemption that came by Christ Jesus. God presented him as a sacrifice of atonement, through faith in his blood. He did this to demonstrate his justice, because in his forbearance he had left the sins committed beforehand unpunished – he did it to demonstrate his justice at the present time, so as to be just and the one who justifies those who have faith in Jesus.

In this passage we find a number of concepts which, taken together, help us to see that Paul's teaching on the atonement can be understood in terms of the controlling metaphor of penal substitution. We must particularly take note of three of these concepts: justification; sacrifice of atonement; and redemption.

'Justification' is a forensic or legal term which describes what God does in transforming our status, through the reconciliation that comes by Christ. Human beings stand guilty before God because of sin. Justification is a proclamation or declaration made by God in which he pardons and accepts guilty sinners. For human beings, this involves a change of status, from being guilty to being pardoned.

'Propitiation' (the New International Version has 'atoning sacrifice') is an expression found in 1 John 2:2 and 4:10. The divine wrath against sin and against sinners had to be dealt with, or propitiated. In some versions, the word 'expiation' is used but this is not a good translation, since 'expiation' is normally used when referring to something impersonal, whereas 'propitiation' is normally used to refer to a personal object, in this case, God. Christ offers a sacrifice to God, to propitiate him, to turn his wrath away from sinners and on to himself. In this way, he takes upon himself the wrath and judgement due to human beings, on account of sin. Propitiation reminds us that when we are thinking about salvation we must remember that there is something on God's side which has to be dealt with as well as the sin on man's side. God's wrath has to be turned away.

The third word in this passage which is of significance to this discussion is 'redemption', meaning to set someone free by paying a price. If you have ever been unfortunate enough to have to pawn something, then you understand this word perfectly! In Paul's day it had all the connotations of the slave market and the idea of a slave being bought out of slavery (or redeemed) into freedom.

Conclusion

If we take all of this together, we can see a consistent argument being put forward that the death of Christ is to be understood as a propitiatory sacrifice in which Christ, as our substitute, took our punishment. By so doing, he provided all that was necessary for our freedom, redemption and justification.

The Theological Argument for Penal Substitution

Introduction

The doctrine of the atonement is part of the unfinished business of Christian theology. The councils and resulting creeds of the early church established the doctrines of the Trinity and the person of Christ in such a way that Catholic, Protestant, Orthodox and most other Christian churches agree on these matters, with relatively minor differences. The atonement, however, is a matter upon which Protestants cannot even agree among themselves. There has been, however, what we might call a central strand of Protestant theology in respect of the atonement, namely, the doctrine of penal substitution. Certainly within the evangelical tradition, this has been the main position held. Nevertheless, many today, even evangelicals, reject this view of the atonement and have sought to put other theories in its place. In this chapter we shall re-examine the doctrine of the atonement and attempt to highlight some areas for further discussion.

Anthropology

Part of the problem for the church is that, in developing any theory of the atonement, an anthropology (a biblical understanding of the human condition) is assumed and it is notoriously difficult to get agreement on the range of issues which comprise a Christian anthropology. It is simply not possible to devise a theory of the atonement without first establishing the nature of the human condition, in order to determine, among other things, why the atonement was necessary and what it was intended to accomplish. We might express the problem in this way: What is the nature of human sin, how is that sin transmitted and how does Christ undo that situation and deal with sin?

Clearly, any theory of the atonement depends upon a theory of human sin. If, on the one hand, we hold to the doctrine of total depravity, with its corresponding commitment to a view of original sin, then that will have implications for how we understand the atonement, since the doctrines of total depravity and original sin pose a specific problem to which the atonement forms part of the answer. If, on the other hand, we hold to a view of humanity in which sin plays little part, then our understanding of the atonement will of necessity be different, since the perceived problem is different. It is also the case that our view of the transmission of sin has implications for our doctrine of the atonement. For example, if we hold that Adam's sin was imputed to humanity and if we hold that it was therefore necessary for Christ's righteousness to be similarly imputed, then we will devise a particular theory of the atonement.

It can easily be seen, then, that alternative theories of the atonement have developed because of alternative anthropologies. Had the church fathers reached an agreed position on sin and its transmission and on Christ's response to this, we might well have had agreement on the atonement but it was not to be. Origen, with his concept of hereditary pollution, came near to a doctrine of original sin, but his speculative neo-Platonism led him to positions which the church ultimately rejected. The doctrine of original sin was developed by Tertullian and others in the Latin West. Even the more basic question as to the origin of souls was disputed between East and West. Greek theology, in so far as it had considered the subject, took a 'creationist' position, that is, each soul is created separately. Tertullian, on the other hand, took a 'traducianist' position, that is, souls result from procreation. Thus Tertullian, while never actually asserting it, paved the way for the doctrine of innate sin. Cyprian, Ambrose and Hilary, in that order, developed this more fully. It was only in response to Pelagius that the entire corruption of both the nature and the will was asserted, and hence prior to Augustine some form of synergism was accepted. Pelagius taught that each person, including Adam, is born in a perfectly free or neutral situation, that is, human beings are neither holy nor inherently evil but have complete freedom to choose between good and evil. There is no imputation of anyone's sin to anyone else, and the widespread evil evident in the world is due to habit, custom and bad example. In response to this, Augustine taught the total depravity of human beings. This expression 'total depravity' does not imply that all human beings are as bad as they could be; rather it means that the 'totality' of the human being is affected by sin, including, for example, the mind and emotions as well as the will. As part of the structure of his response, Augustine also taught a clear view as to the transmission of sin.

Theories of atonement

These various developing understandings of anthropology had their counterparts in various theories of atonement. In the era of the apostolic fathers, however, there was little in the way of systematic statement. They spoke in scriptural language about the death of Christ, without speculating on a possible framework in which to comprehend this language. In the Epistle to Diognetus we have sin as deserving punishment and Christ as the ransom for sin but without further reflection or argument. In Marcion, the ransom is paid by the God of the New Testament to the God of the Old Testament. This was rejected as heresy but other writers, like Origen, argued that the ransom was paid to Satan. L.W. Grensted argues that the notion of ransom to the devil 'remained the customary and orthodox statement of the doctrine of the Atonement for nearly a thousand years.'[1] Ultimately this too was rejected by the church.

Tertullian coined the theological vocabulary which was destined to become the future 'grammar' of the doctrine of atonement. His intensely legal mind formulated a system centering on 'satisfaction' and 'merit'. Augustine added little but changed this anthropological emphasis to a more Christological one. Gregory the Great draws these threads together, speaking of Christ as Redeemer and Mediator, that is, the angry God being propitiated by a sacrifice which, in the nature of things, had to be both God and man.[2] Irenaeus was the first to relate the atonement to the justice of God although not in the subsequent language of Tertullian. He also stressed the theory of 'recapitulation', whereby Christ undid the damage which sin had done to the human condition, in all its ages and stages. Hence he became a child to sanctify our childhood, a man to sanctify our adulthood and so on. This is

---

[1] L.W. Grensted, *A Short History of the Doctrine of the Atonement* (London: Manchester University Press, 1920), p. 56.
[2] See R. Seeberg, *Text-book of the History of Doctrines* (Grand Rapids, MI: Baker, 1958), vol. 2, pp. 19ff.

not the same as the active obedience of Christ to the law in his role as the second (or last) Adam, but it is a somewhat parallel argument.

In Athanasius' *De Incarnatione Verbi* (On the Incarnation of the Word) we have the first systematic statement of the nature of the atonement.[3] He taught that Christ endured the wrath of God as a penalty on our behalf, although he maintained that this sacrifice was made to the honour or veracity of God and not to his justice. Anselm was the first to speak of the logical necessity of the atonement, it previously having been generally viewed as an act of God's will which originated out of a choice from a number of possible alternatives, not excluding the possibility of forgiveness without atonement. He follows Athanasius in holding that the atonement is made to the honour of God and indeed specifically rejects penal interpretations.[4] Anselm believed that punishment and satisfaction were logical alternatives, that is, if satisfaction were not made to the divine honour then mankind must be eternally punished.[5] The Reformers argued that these were not opposites but rather complementary, that is, Christ received from the Father the punishment due to sinners, while making satisfaction.

Another view of the atonement received classic expression in the work of Abelard, that is, the 'moral influence' or exemplarist theory. The death of Christ at Calvary becomes not an element in a juridical transaction but rather a great example of self-sacrifice, designed to highlight God's love and to bring humanity to the place of repentance and obedience. Aquinas presented a synthesis of Anselmic and Abelardian theories, but the Reformers returned to an exposition of the former, while rejecting Anselm's concept of the logical necessity of atonement. The Reformers, especially Calvin, placed great emphasis on Christ as 'victim' or 'lamb for the slaughter'. At the same time, however, Luther envisioned Christ as 'victor' defeating the powers of evil, a view later spelled out in more detail by Gustaf Aulen[6] and recently reappropriated in an important work by Hans Boersma.[7]

---

[3] Athanasius, *De Incarnatione Verbi*, in *St Athanasius: Select Works and Letters*, A Select Library of Nicene and Post-Nicene Fathers of the Christian Church, series 2, vol. 4 (ed. P. Schaff and H. Wace; Grand Rapids, MI: Eerdmans, 1980), pp. 31-67.

[4] Anselm, *Cur Deus Homo* (London: Religious Tract Society, no date), Book II, section XVIII, part 2.

[5] Ibid, Book I, section XIII.

[6] Gustaf Aulen, *Christus Victor* (London: Macmillan, 1934).

[7] Hans Boersma, *Violence, Hospitality, and the Cross* (Grand Rapids, MI: Baker, 2004).

Federal theology and the atonement

The Reformers' emphasis on (and modification of) Anselm was further
honed by those who followed in the Reformed tradition, within the
context of 'federal theology', as represented by such documents as the
Westminster Confession of Faith. This view comprises a certain position
in respect of the nature and transmission of sin, with a corresponding
position regarding the nature of Christ's sacrifice and the transmission
of his righteousness. Here we can see clearly the implications of an
anthropology for the doctrine of the atonement.

In expounding the federal view, we must first distinguish between
the Augustinian view of sin and the federal view of sin. It is best
explained by saying that Augustine held to the 'natural headship' of
Adam whereas the federal theologians hold to the 'federal headship'
of Adam. The Augustinian theory is that God imputes the sin (singu-
lar, being only the first sin) of Adam to his posterity:

> in virtue of that organic unity of mankind by which the whole race at the
> time of Adam's transgression existed, not individually, but seminally, in
> him as its head . . . In Adam's free act, the will of the race revolted from
> God and the nature of the race corrupted itself. The nature which we now
> possess is the same nature that corrupted itself in Adam.[8]

For the Augustinian, it is morally reprehensible to suggest guilt without
direct involvement in the sin, and hence it is taught that we are not guilty
because of Adam's sin but because of our own. As G.P. Fisher writes:

> The fundamental idea of the Augustinian theory is that of a participation
> on the part of the descendants of Adam in his first sin; in consequence of
> which they are born both guilty and morally depraved. The fundamen-
> tal idea of the federal theory is that of a vicarious representation on the
> part of Adam, in virtue of a covenant between God and him, whereby
> the legal responsibility for his first sinful act is entailed upon all his
> descendants; participation being excluded, but the propriety of his
> appointment to this vicarious office being founded on our relation to him
> as the common father of men.[9]

---

[8] A.H. Strong, *Systematic Theology* (Philadelphia: American Baptist Publication
Society, 1907), vol. 2, p. 619.
[9] 'The Augustinian and the Federal Theories of Original Sin Compared', *New
Englander* (July 1868), pp. 469–516.

When we come to Anselm we see an important development. Like Augustine, he saw Adam as the natural head of a generic type, but was more definite about imputation, by arguing that humanity after the fall is polluted by sin and, as such, guilty. Both the guilt and the pollution are passed on from parent to child. The criticism normally raised against this view is that it implies that the sins of our parents and other ancestors are imputed to us. As Louis Berkhof noted, 'This is undoubtedly a weak point in the system of Anselm, since all the following sins are committed by the same nature, though individualised, and because it does not answer the question, why only the first sin of Adam is imputed to his posterity, and not his later sins.'[10] The post-Reformation theologians developed the covenant idea as a more exact way of speaking about the relationship between Adam's sin and our depravity. Between Calvin and the end of the seventeenth century, the federal system was elaborated in all its complexity.[11]

Federal theology (or covenant theology) taught that the key to understanding God's dealings with humanity is the 'covenant' concept. The argument is that in Genesis 2:16,17 God made a 'covenant of works' with Adam whereby life was promised to him on condition of perfect obedience, particularly to the command of God not to eat from the tree of the knowledge of good and evil. In this covenant Adam was not envisaged merely as a private individual, but as the representative head of all humanity or, to put it another way, the 'federal head' of the race. Hence we were all 'in Adam' when the covenant was made, not merely generically but federally. This being the case, when Adam broke the covenant, the judgement fell upon all those who had been representatively involved, namely, all humanity. Thus original sin comes to each person by the 'imputation' of Adam's sin.

Humanity being in the fallen state, God promises a 'covenant of grace' (so the federal theologians understood the *protoevangelion* of Genesis 3:15) which he duly instigated with Abraham (Genesis 12 and 15), who was promised life for himself and his descendants not on the condition of perfect obedience but by grace. God could not merely ignore his own righteousness and justice, however, and so in order to

---

[10] Louis Berkhof, *The History of Christian Doctrines* (London: Banner of Truth, 1937), p. 143.

[11] D.A. Weir, *The Origins of the Federal Theology in Sixteenth-Century Reformation Thought* (Oxford: Clarendon, 1990); Charles S. McCoy and J. Wayne Baker, *Fountainhead of Federalism: Heinrich Bullinger and the Covenantal Tradition* (Louisville, KY: Westminster/John Knox, 1991).

forgive sinners there had to be a satisfaction made. This was to be in the form of a sacrifice as 'typified' by the ceremonial law. In what then did this consist? God elected some certain individuals out of the mass of fallen humanity and made a covenant with them in Christ their federal head, promising them eternal life on condition that Christ fulfilled the requirements of the covenant. This involved, on the one hand, a life of perfect obedience, succeeding where Adam had failed (his active obedience) and, on the other hand, death on the cross, offering himself as a penal substitutionary sacrifice to atone for the sins of the elect (his passive obedience).

It is this penal substitutionary view of the atonement which became the dominant view in Reformed theology and to which we must now turn.

Penal substitution

In 1974 the *Tyndale Bulletin* published J.I. Packer's Tyndale Biblical Theology Lecture, which had been delivered in July 1973 and was entitled 'What Did the Cross Achieve? The Logic of Penal Substitution'.[12] In the interim years, that published article has been recognized as something of a classic statement of the nature of the atonement.

Over thirty years later, it is useful to reflect on that lecture and on the changes that have taken place in attitudes towards this doctrine since then. In order to do this, we shall first review Packer's original lecture, highlighting its main argument. Second, we shall consider the range of views today concerning penal substitution. Third, we shall review a recent essay on the atonement by J.I. Packer, in order to see if there have been any changes in, or developments of, his view in the past thirty years.

The logic of penal substitution

J.I. Packer began his 1973 lecture by identifying his purpose, namely, 'to focus and explicate a belief which, by and large, is a distinguishing mark of the word-wide [sic] evangelical fraternity: namely, the

---

[12] J.I. Packer, 'What Did the Cross Achieve? The Logic of Penal Substitution', *TynBul* 25 (1974): pp. 3–45.

belief that Christ's death on the cross had the character of *penal sub-stitution* . . .'[13] In the light of what we shall see later, it is striking that, only thirty years ago, Packer was able to identify penal substitution as a 'distinguishing feature' of evangelicalism. This was no peripheral issue where a range of views might legitimately be expected but one which lay at the heart of what it meant to be an evangelical. It is also interesting to note Packer's analysis of the history of the doctrine, indicating that the main proponents of penal substitution were the magisterial Reformers and that the main opposition came from Socinus and other Unitarian theologians. It is also illuminating to note that the arguments used against penal substitution by Socinus included the charges that it was 'irrational, incoherent, immoral and impossible'.[14] These same criticisms of the doctrine, as we shall see, are used today by some who lay claim to being evangelical. The theological landscape, then, has changed quite dramatically in thirty years.

Penal substitution, as defined by Packer, is the belief that Christ, on our behalf, underwent 'vicarious punishment (*poena*) to meet the claims on us of God's holy law and wrath (*i.e.* his punitive justice).'[15] It must be noted, however, that Packer is not prepared to defend every exposition of penal substitution, or at least every method of stating and defending it. Indeed, he is quite critical of what he calls 'methodological rationalism'[16] and names Turretin, A.A. Hodge and Berkhof as having fallen into this trap.[17] He writes:

> Their stance was defensive rather than declaratory, analytical and apologetic rather than doxological and kerygmatic. They made the word of the cross sound more like a conundrum than a confession of faith – more like a puzzle, we might say, than a gospel. What was happening? Just this: that in trying to beat Socinian rationalism at its own game, Reformed theologians were conceding the Socinian assumption that every aspect of God's work of reconciliation will be exhaustively explicable in terms of a natural theology of divine government, drawn from the world of contemporary legal and political thought. Thus, in their zeal to show themselves rational, they became rationalistic.[18]

[13] Ibid, p. 3. The 'word-wide' evangelical fraternity is an interesting typographical error!
[14] Ibid, p. 4.
[15] Ibid, p. 4.
[16] Ibid, p. 5.
[17] Ibid, pp. 4–5.
[18] Ibid, p. 5.

In response to these writers, Packer says that we should not be afraid to speak of 'mystery' and to have unsolved problems in our theology.[19] This is simply a recognition that we are creatures and that we cannot exhaustively know the mind of God. He takes this further by noting the inherent problem of using human language to express divine realities,[20] except by means of 'parables, analogies, metaphors and images'.[21] To drive this point home, he argues that the traditional method of Christian theology is to take biblical models and to build our doctrinal systems on the basis of these models, which then act as 'controls'. He illustrates this with reference to scientific method: 'As models in physics are hypotheses formed under the suggestive control of empirical evidence to correlate and predict phenomena, so Christian theological models are explanatory constructs formed to help us know, understand and deal with God, the ultimate reality.'[22] The final strand of what he calls his 'methodological preliminaries'[23] is to indicate his doctrine of Scripture, what he calls 'the mainstream Christian belief in biblical inspiration'.[24] He is quite clear that knowledge and understanding of the meaning of the cross can only come from one source. He writes, 'By what means is knowledge of the mystery of the cross given us? I reply: through the didactic thought-models given in the Bible, which in truth are instructions from God.'[25] This affirmation is identical to that of another significant Reformed writer on the atonement, John Murray, who says, 'There is only one source from which we can derive a proper conception of Christ's atoning work. That source is the Bible. There is only one norm by which our interpretations and formulations are to be tested. That norm is the Bible. The temptation ever lurks near us to prove unfaithful to this one and only criterion.'[26]

Packer then moves into the first main theme of his paper and deals with the concept of 'substitution'.[27] He argues that substitution means

---

[19] Ibid, pp. 7–8.

[20] Ibid, pp. 8–11.

[21] Ibid, p. 10.

[22] Ibid, p. 12.

[23] Ibid, p. 16.

[24] Ibid, p. 13.

[25] Idem.

[26] John Murray, *Redemption Accomplished and Applied* (London: Banner of Truth, 1961), p. 76.

[27] J.I. Packer, 'What Did the Cross Achieve? The Logic of Penal Substitution', *TynBul* 25 (1974): pp. 16–25.

taking the place of another and includes the concept of vicarious representation, which some had seen as an alternative.[28] He is quite clear that this concept of substitution is soundly based in Scripture, not least in Paul's statement in Romans 5:8 that 'Christ died for us', taken together with Paul's other statement in Galatians 3:13 that 'Christ redeemed us from the curse of the law, having become a curse for us.'[29] Packer notes that this idea of substitution was almost wholly rejected by British theologians of the time but that Barth and Pannenberg affirmed it.[30] In defending his argument for substitution, Packer notes that, in the history of the church, there have been essentially three ways of viewing the atonement. First, to say that it has effect entirely upon human beings, for example, as an example of self-sacrificial love which we ought to follow; second, to argue that the atonement is directed primarily at 'hostile spiritual forces'; or third, to say that the atonement includes both of these concepts but is primarily directed at God on our behalf. Packer argues for the third of these positions.

He then moves on to argue the case for adding the word 'penal' to that of 'substitution', in order to clarify the nature and intent of the substitution. He says that to add this word 'is to anchor the model of substitution (not exclusively but regulatively) within the world of moral law, guilty conscience, and retributive justice. Thus is forged a conceptual instrument for conveying the thought that God remits our sins and accepts our persons into favour not because of any amends we have attempted, but because the penalty which was our due was diverted on to Christ.'[31]

Rather than re-presenting traditional constructs of penal substitution, Packer devises his own and that for several reasons. First, he wishes to avoid ways of presenting the subject which are unhelpful, both those he calls 'devotionally evocative without always being theologically rigorous'[32] and those rationalistic constructs mentioned above which are essentially responses to Socinus on his own terms. Second, he wishes to highlight penal substitution's character as both dramatic and kerygmatic. Third, he wants to avoid the charge that penal substitution is impersonal and abstract. He is keen to demonstrate that, seen properly, it is truly moral, personal and relational.[33]

---

[28] Particularly P.T. Forsyth, ibid, pp. 22–3.
[29] Ibid, p. 17.
[30] Ibid, p. 19.
[31] Ibid, p. 25.
[32] Idem.
[33] Ibid, pp. 25–9.

There follows an extensive analysis of various scriptural passages which indicate that Christ bore the wrath of God on our behalf, under five themes: 'substitution and retribution; substitution and solidarity; substitution and mystery; substitution and salvation; substitution and divine love.'[34] Packer's conclusion is that penal substitution is 'the heart of the matter.'[35] Or, as he puts it earlier in his argument:

> This analysis, if correct, shows what job the word 'penal' does in our model. It is there, not to prompt theoretical puzzlement about the transferring of guilt, but to articulate the insight of believers who, as they look at Calvary in the light of the New Testament, are constrained to say, 'Jesus was bearing the judgement I deserved (and deserve), the penalty for my sins, the punishment due to me' – 'he loved me, and gave himself for me' (Gal. 2:20). How it was possible for him to bear their penalty they do not claim to know, and no more than they know how it was possible for him to be made man; but that he bore it is the certainty on which all their hopes rest.[36]

In my view, Packer's understanding of this doctrine is soundly based on Scripture and remains a definitive statement of the teaching of Scripture.

Recent views on penal substitution

When Packer wrote his lecture, the boundary lines, as he saw it, were clear. On the one hand, there were those who rejected the notion of penal substitution, largely those adhering to traditional Liberal Theology, represented by scholars like Vincent Taylor and F.W. Camfield, but also including some who were evangelical in other aspects of their theology but who denied some aspect of penal substitution, like P.T. Forsyth. On the other hand, there were those who supported penal substitution, identified as the world-wide community of evangelicals.

Today, the situation is much more complex. In order to demonstrate this complexity, I want to indicate some of those who today reject penal substitution, noting that this group now includes some who would claim to be evangelical.

---

[34] Ibid, pp. 29–43.
[35] Ibid, p. 45.
[36] Ibid, p. 31.

The remnants of old liberal theology

The annual meeting of the Society for the Study of Theology which took place in Newcastle in April 2003 had as its theme 'The Cross'. Many different aspects of the atonement were dealt with but it was notable that no-one argued in favour of the traditional exposition of penal substitution, which can surely lay legitimate claim to being regarded as part of the mainstream tradition of atonement theology. For example, Peter Selby's presidential address focussed on themes of social justice and Mary Grey argued for an ecological understanding of the implications of Christian theology. Like the others, Clive Marsh and Rita Nakashima Brock were fairly dismissive of traditional views of atonement, not least because of their feminist or womanist perspectives. Even Kathryn Tanner, who sought to argue for an incarnational understanding of the atonement, rejected notions of penal substitution, although she then struggled to explain what precisely it was that the death of Christ contributed to salvation, as over against that which had already been accomplished in the incarnation.

Most interesting, however, was the apparent consensus that the Bible did contain a doctrine of penal substitution but that we know better today and ought to dismiss it in favour of other models. These other models may be ones which we create ourselves, since we are not bound by the biblical models. In other words, the issue with this group remains the authority of Scripture. Are we free to abandon models which are central to Scripture, just because they are inconsistent with the cultural consensus of the early twenty-first century? Many of these theologians would appear to answer 'yes'.

Radical theology especially feminist theology

These scholars, however, were relatively mild in their critique of traditional views of the atonement compared to Daphne Hampson, whose position is much more radical and thoroughgoing than those just mentioned.[37] Having herself abandoned Christianity, she argues strongly that it is immoral, not least because of the way it has treated women. On the particular matter of sacrifice, she dismisses any notion of the Father punishing the Son as 'pernicious' since it involves a religious symbolism which can be used to justify violence against children by fathers. She appears to quote approvingly Rita

---

[37] Daphne Hampson, *After Christianity* (London: SCM, 2002).

Nakashima Brock's dismissal of penal substitution as cosmic 'child abuse.'[38]

What I want to note, however, is that for her also the key issue is revelation. At various points in her argument, she is quite dismissive of 'Christian feminists', viewing them as largely inconsistent and having not worked through the implications of their theology. For example, she writes, 'Why anyone who calls herself (or himself) a feminist, who believes in human equality, should wish to hold to a patriarchal myth such as Christianity must remain a matter for bafflement.'[39] She continues to regard herself as a theist, however, since she believes that there is a dimension to reality which she calls 'God'. This reality, however, is not a personal being who is 'outside' or 'beyond' history as we know it.

On the person and work of Christ, Hampson struggles to identify any meaning which would be compatible with post-Enlightenment thought. She insists that the key problem in Christianity is its claim to be unique and to be historical in the sense of rooted in a specific, revelatory space/time event. She notes, 'What it is never necessary to do, given the religious position which I espouse, is to measure what one would say against some benchmark in history. For I am denying that there has been any particular revelation in history with which one should compare what one wishes to think.'[40] And again, 'The problem with Christianity is that Christians hold that there has been a revelation in history, so that the past becomes a necessary point of reference. That is heteronomous. It is not how we think today. We need to take responsibility for our ethical stance and, equally, for our spirituality.'[41]

She is also dismissive of liberal scholars, who try to retain Christianity by demythologizing this concept of history:

> In response I must insist that if Christianity is called a 'historical' religion simply in the sense that Christians are part of a continuous history which reaches back to Jesus of Nazareth . . . as though being a Christian consisted in nothing more than siting oneself within a certain tradition, something essential has been lost. The decisive point about Christianity has always been (and surely always must be) that Christians believe there to have been a revelation in Christ. That in different ages

---

[38] Ibid, pp. 151–2.
[39] Ibid, p. 50.
[40] Ibid, p. 57.
[41] Ibid, p. 83.

Christians have spoken in different terms of the uniqueness which is the implication of such a revelation is certainly the case. But Christianity is not just 'historical' in the sense that historically it had its origin in the life, death and teaching of one particular man. Being Christian cannot be held to mean no more than being part of a particular community, like being English.[42]

She is also highly critical of all supposedly Christian scholarship which seeks to retain commitment to Christianity while rejecting its traditional Christological claims.

I think, then, that one must round on the suggestion that what is rightly to be called a Christology could fail to make any claim to there having been a uniqueness. In the first place that is not congruent with what Christians have always believed. From the earliest days Christians have not simply proclaimed Jesus' message, but a kerygma, a message, about Jesus. To repeat what I said earlier: either the Christ event is shattering, or it is nothing. If it is nothing – that is to say, Jesus was just a rather fine human being and that is the end of the matter – then one can take or leave him as one will. No one who is Christian could possibly assent to such a proposition! Christianity is a religion for which people have died as martyrs – not inconsistently if it is true.[43]

This is a fascinating point. She is saying that liberal theologians and Christian feminists who seek to retain the language and liturgy of Christianity, while rejecting its content, are essentially being inconsistent and perhaps even dishonest! Her rejection of a traditional view of the atonement, then, is part and parcel of her rejection of Christianity as a whole and more specifically her rejection of the uniqueness of Jesus Christ as the God-man.

The neo-orthodox

If liberal theologians reject penal substitution because they have rejected the authority of Scripture and radicals like Daphne Hampson reject penal substitution because they have rejected Christianity, this third group reject penal substitution because they believe it to be inconsistent with an orthodox doctrine of God.

---

[42] Ibid, p. 42.
[43] Ibid, p. 43.

Barth argues strongly in favour of using the word 'substitution' in respect of our redemption. It is, however, important to note two things. First, that the word translated as 'substitution' (*Stellvertretung*) incorporates the ideas of both substitution and representation.[44] Second, that when Barth uses the word 'substitution', 'it is given a sense more radical than is normally the case in English, because Barth envisages it as a total displacement of sinful man by the incarnate, crucified and risen Son; and also more comprehensive, because it is related to the whole life and work of Jesus Christ, including His heavenly intercession.'[45]

What is also clear, however, is that Barth and those who have followed in his footsteps reject the concept of 'penal' substitution, preferring instead to argue for an incarnational understanding of redemption. That is to say, he argues that the very act of the Word becoming flesh involved reconciliation. God, in the person of the Son, takes to himself a (fallen) human nature and thus, in the very person of Christ, God and humanity are reconciled. Effectively the judgement of God is taken upon God himself.[46] Salvation is no longer to be seen in the forensic terms of the courtroom, whereby Christ, by a substitutionary action, obtains a benefit which is then passed on to others. Rather, salvation is to be found in the very being of Christ and therefore union with Christ becomes the key doctrine. Once we are united to Christ we share in his reconciled humanity and so receive all of the blessings which God delights to pour out upon us. This obviates the need for penal substitution and the subsequent conferral of the benefits of Christ's death upon sinners.[47] In an important article, Trevor Hart spells out the implications of this for justification.[48] He critiques both traditional Protestant and traditional Roman Catholic views as teaching the notion of 'benefits' being obtained, rather than viewing justification Christologically.

If asked to identify an alternative model for understanding the atonement, most in this group would offer support for John McLeod

---

[44] See Karl Barth, *Church Dogmatics* IV/ I (ET ed. G.W. Bromiley and T.F. Torrance; Edinburgh: T&T Clark, 1936–9), pp. vii–viii.

[45] Idem.

[46] Barth, *Church Dogmatics* IV/ I, pp. 211–83.

[47] This is appropriately the great theme of the festschrift for James B. Torrance: *Christ in Our Place: The Humanity of God in Christ for the Reconciliation of the World* (ed. Trevor Hart and Daniel Thimell; Exeter: Paternoster, 1989).

[48] Trevor Hart, 'Humankind in Christ and Christ in Humankind: Salvation as Participation in Our Substitute in the Theology of John Calvin', *SJT* 42 (1989): pp. 67-74. See also 'Justification: Barth, Trent, and Küng', *SJT* 34:6 (1981): pp. 517–29.

Campbell, who rejected the *Westminster Confession of Faith*'s penal substitutionary view of the atonement with its accompanying commitment to particular redemption, and developed his theory of 'vicarious repentance'. In this view, the incarnation and not the atonement is the key event and the love of God to all humanity is the key *motif*. As Ian Hamilton notes, 'The atonement is made not by Christ suffering vicariously the wrath of God for sinners, but by Christ's perfect confession and repentance of sin . . .'[49]

Barth's Christological methodology and his incarnational understanding of atonement do not themselves, however, take us to the heart of his problem with respect to penal substitution. The key problem lies in the doctrine of God. The problem might be expressed in this way: How could it possibly be that the Father should punish the Son? Would this not involve an inner-Trinitarian breach, which is surely unthinkable?

This can be illustrated by referring to a sermon preached by an evangelical minister. In the course of his sermon he noted the word of Jesus from the cross, 'My God, my God, why have you forsaken me?' He immediately said that, of course, Jesus was not *truly* abandoned; he only *felt* abandoned. I wanted to say, 'No, he truly was abandoned.' In other words, I wanted to argue that in some mysterious way, there takes place a breach within the inner councils of the Trinity at that moment on the cross because the divine Son, who has taken to himself a human nature, has become sin and is bearing the wrath of God for sin.

In pressing for the reality of the Father's punishing of the Son, however, one important qualification has to be made. Even in the midst of that great transaction on the cross, the Father never ceased to love the Son and to be well pleased with him. This was a point that Calvin stressed:

> Yet we do not suggest that God was ever inimical or angry toward him. How could he be angry toward his beloved Son, 'in whom his heart reposed' [cf. Matthew 3:17]? How could Christ by his intercession appease the Father toward others, if he were himself hateful to God? This is what we are saying: he bore the weight of divine severity, since he was 'stricken and afflicted' [cf. Isaiah 53:5] by God's hand, and experienced all the signs of a wrathful and avenging God.[50]

---

[49] 'John McLeod Campbell', in *New Dictionary of Theology* (ed. S.B. Ferguson and D.F. Wright; Leicester: IVP, 1988).

[50] John Calvin, *Institutes*, 2/16/11.

In other words, the Father was not hostile to the Son in and of himself, even though Christ 'bore the weight of divine severity'. This is essentially the same point which was made by George Smeaton, when he wrote that Christ:

> endured divine wrath, that is, the divine desertion, as the Mediator between God and man, subjecting Himself to all that had devolved upon humanity as the curse of sin. His substitution was not, indeed, identity. He could therefore be the object of the divine wrath in our place, while still the beloved Son and the sinless man. He was made sin while sinlessly perfect and accepted: He was made a curse while yet the faultless servant: He was the object of true punishment, and of all that goes to constitute true wrath, as He stood in our place to bear what was due to us for sin, while in Himself the Son of His love (Col. i.13), and the approved and accepted second Adam, and never more the object of His approval that when he offered Himself for others (John x.17). We draw the distinction between the personal and the official.[51]

Let me say that I understand the difficulty which attaches to this subject of the Son bearing the wrath of the Father and I fully respect the theological complexity that is involved in maintaining penal substitution in the light of the need for a careful delineating of the relationship between the Father and the Son. In my view, this is the strongest theological argument to be faced by any doctrine of penal substitution.

There is, however, an alternative view of Barth, namely, that he can be viewed as a significant defender of penal substitution, albeit in a redefined manner. Bruce McCormack of Princeton University, in an article in the festschrift for Roger Nicole, outlines a way of reinstating penal substitution and defending it against its detractors by using Karl Barth's ontology![52] Essentially, his argument is that the opponents of penal substitution have been successful in their arguments because, in most of the Reformed tradition, the doctrine of penal substitution has been defined in ways which demonstrate an inadequate

---

[51] George Smeaton, *The Apostles' Doctrine of the Atonement* (Edinburgh: Banner of Truth, 1991), p. 314.

[52] Bruce L. McCormack, 'The Ontological Presuppositions of Barth's Doctrine of the Atonement', in *The Glory of the Atonement: Biblical, Historical and Practical Perspectives* (ed. Charles E. Hill and Frank A. James III; Downers Grove, IL: IVP, 2004), pp. 346–66.

Christology and an inadequate doctrine of the Trinity. Once these problems are solved, however, a doctrine of penal substitution can be developed which is not subject to the normal criticisms levelled against it.

McCormack writes:

> The subject who delivers Jesus Christ up to death is not the Father alone. For the Trinitarian axiom opera trinitatis ad extra sunt indivisa means that if one does it, they all do it. So it is the triune God (Father, Son and Holy Spirit) who gives himself over to this experience. And that also means, then, that the Father is not doing something to some- one other than himself. The triune God pours his wrath out upon him- self in and through the human nature that he has made his own in his second mode of his being – that is the ontological significance of penal substitution. The triune God takes this human experience into his own life; he 'drinks it to the dregs.' And in doing so, he vanquishes its power over us. That, I would submit, is the meaning of penal substitution when seen against the background of a well-ordered Christology and a well-ordered doctrine of the Trinity.[53]

What we have to decide, of course, is whether this reconstruction of the doctrine of penal substitution saves the doctrine from its detrac- tors, or empties it of some of the significance accorded to it in the Scriptures.

Revisionist evangelicals

We must now draw attention to the fact that a number of those who would normally be regarded as mainstream evangelicals and who hold to evangelical views on most subjects, as identified, for example, by such documents as the Basis of Faith of the Evangelical Alliance, have now departed from a belief in penal substitution.

One interesting feature of this group is that they come to the same conclusion as the above-noted liberal theologians but for very differ- ent reasons. The liberals say that penal substitution is taught in Scripture but we are not bound by that. These evangelicals either say that the Bible does not teach penal substitution, or they say that penal substitution is only one model among many and therefore ought not to be the controlling interpretive theme in our theology of atonement.

---

[53] Ibid, p. 364.

Let me give three examples of this group.

Green and Baker
The evangelical credentials of Joel Green and Mark Baker are not in doubt, yet in a recent volume, *Recovering the Scandal of the Cross*,[54] they deny the notion of penal substitution. Many have hailed this book as an important contribution and, indeed, it has received strong commendations from various well-known evangelicals.

The core argument put forward by Green and Baker is that what we have in the New Testament is a range of models for understanding the atonement. In this respect their argument is similar to that of Colin Gunton.[55] They go further, however, in arguing that the writers of the New Testament were not presenting models for all time but looking for models which would be understood by the specific communities to whom they were speaking. This means that we today must be developing models which speak to our own communities and societies, seeing the biblical models as examples rather than as solid and final parameters for our doctrine. Their desire to see new models developed, however, is coupled with a specific rejection of the model of penal substitution. As they say in their conclusion, 'We believe that the popular fascination with and commitment to penal substitutionary atonement has had ill effects in the life of the church in the United States and has little to offer the global church and mission by way of understanding or embodying the message of Jesus Christ.'[56]

St John's versus Oak Hill
A second example of evangelicals rejecting penal substitution is represented by the dispute between two Anglican colleges traditionally regarded as evangelical: St John's Nottingham and Oak Hill College, London. This began with the publication in 1995 of the papers from a symposium on the atonement, which had taken place at St John's.[57] Some of the contributors rejected the connection between atonement and punishment (John Goldingay and Stephen Travis) whereas others

---

[54] Joel B. Green and Mark D. Baker, *Recovering the Scandal of the Cross: Atonement in New Testament and Contemporary Contexts* (Carlisle: Paternoster, 2000).

[55] Colin E. Gunton, *The Actuality of Atonement: A Study of Metaphor, Rationality and the Christian Tradition* (Edinburgh: T&T Clark, 1988).

[56] Green and Baker, *Scandal of the Cross*, pp. 220–21.

[57] John Goldingay, ed., *Atonement Today* (London: SPCK, 1995).

reinterpreted the words 'penal substitution' and used them in a different way (Christina Baxter and Tom Smail).

The response came in the form of the published papers from another symposium, namely, the Fourth Oak Hill College Annual School of Theology.[58] Here we have an unequivocal defence of penal substitution, with an extensive analysis of biblical texts by David Peterson and theological articles by Garry Williams and others. Clearly this debate highlights a major fault line within evangelical theology, not least in mainstream denominations.

Steve Chalke

The third example is perhaps the most striking because, although over the years some evangelical theologians have rejected the notion of penal substitution, it has largely remained the standard view among popular evangelical writers. This recently changed when Steve Chalke, of Oasis Trust, argued against penal substitution.[59] His objection to penal substitution, and to some other evangelical beliefs, is on the basis of a general principle concerning God's love. For example, on the question of God telling his people Israel to engage in battle against their enemies, as recorded in the Old Testament, he says that this was not true to God's character and implies that the people of Israel either misunderstood or misrepresented God. He writes:

> Yahweh's association with vengeance and violence wasn't so much an expression of who he was but the result of his determination to be involved with his world. His unwillingness to distance himself from the people of Israel and their actions meant that at times he was implicated in the excessive acts of war that we see in some of the books of the Old Testament. From the very beginning, Yahweh's dealings with Israel were motivated by his desire to demonstrate his love. But to a people saturated in a worldview that saw him as power, this was always going to be a slow uphill struggle.[60]

His determination to vindicate God from anything which early twenty-first-century people might find unpalatable includes the following

---

[58] David Peterson, ed., *Where Wrath and Mercy Meet: Proclaiming the Atonement Today* (Carlisle: Paternoster, 2001).

[59] Steve Chalke and Alan Mann, *The Lost Message of Jesus* (Grand Rapids, MI: Zondervan, 2003).

[60] Ibid, p. 49.

statement: 'The Bible . . . never makes assertions about [God's] anger, power or judgement independently of his love.'[61] He does not attempt to justify this statement exegetically.

He explains his core working principle in this same section of the book when he writes, 'The fact is, however else God may have revealed himself, and in whatever way he interacts with the world he has created, everything is to be tempered, interpreted, understood and seen through the one, primary lens of God's love.'[62] He does not seek to justify this statement beyond arguing that the statement 'God is love' is paradigmatic.

He further subverts the traditional evangelical view by denying the doctrine of original sin. He writes:

> To see humanity as inherently evil and steeped in original sin instead of inherently made in God's image and so bathed in original goodness, however hidden it may have become, is a serious mistake. It is this grave error that has dogged the Church in the West for centuries. In the fourth century Augustine developed his influential theology that the material world and everything in it was inherently evil and corrupt. This 'fallenness' he said, was like a virus, and in humans was passed on through the act of sexual intercourse and conception. So from the seeds of Augustine's thinking, the doctrine of original sin was born. However, the Eastern Church instead followed the teaching of Irenaeus, who believed that all people were God's-image bearers and though flawed were, as he put it, like flowers in bud – slowly coaxed into full bloom by God's love.[63]

In the course of developing his argument Chalke makes some quite dramatic claims. He argues that Jesus came to 'declare war on' the Temple and that 'in effect, he was announcing that it was redundant, irrelevant and obsolete'.[64] This is not argued in the context of Christ's once-for-all sacrifice making unnecessary the sacrificial system established in the Old Testament but as part of Jesus' ministry during his life.

He also says that 'when it comes to the God of the Bible there is only one kind of sin in the world – forgiven sin.'[65] This is said in the

[61] Ibid, p. 63.
[62] Ibid.
[63] Ibid, p. 67.
[64] Ibid, p. 105.
[65] Ibid, p. 109.

context of the parable of the prodigal son but no theological rationale is given for the continued existence of unforgiven sin, nor for the continued existence of those who reject Christ.

In opposition to the view that someone is either a Christian or not a Christian, having either been born again or not born again, he quotes approvingly from C.S. Lewis who believed that no such clear divide existed.[66] In driving this point home, he notes that Jesus only used the expression 'you must be born again' twice, in one conversation with Nicodemus, and then goes on to say, 'And yet it has become the basis for one of the most confused, misused and abused, misunderstood and despised ideas in the history of the Church.'[67] He writes:

> The truth is that when Jesus spoke to Nicodemus (a sincere, questioning and spiritually seeking Pharisee), he was not using the term 'born again' in the same sense we have come to do. Jesus was simply saying that entering into God's Kingdom or shalom is about seeing the world differently and adopting his new agenda. It is about dropping the crushing, life-draining, religious dogma and discovering the freedom that God loves you as you are and that his Kingdom is available to you.[68]

Just in case we have not yet grasped the point he says, 'for John, being born-again wasn't the crisis experience we have made it'.[69]

With this background, then, it is no surprise that when he comes to deal with the atonement, he also rejects the traditional evangelical position. He writes:

> John's Gospel famously declares, 'God loved the people of this world so much that he gave his only Son' (John 3:16). How then, have we come to believe that at the cross this God of love suddenly decides to vent his anger and wrath on his own Son? The fact is that the cross isn't a form of cosmic child abuse – a vengeful Father, punishing his Son for an offence he has not even committed. Understandably, both people inside and outside of the Church have found this twisted version of events morally dubious and a huge barrier to faith. Deeper than that, however, is that such a concept stands in total contradiction to the statement 'God is love'. If the cross is a

---

[66] Ibid, p. 141.
[67] Ibid, p. 147.
[68] Ibid, p. 148.
[69] Ibid, p. 149.

personal act of violence perpetrated by God towards humankind but borne by his Son, then it makes a mockery of Jesus' own teaching to love your enemies and to refuse to repay evil with evil. The truth is, the cross is a symbol of love. It is a demonstration of just how far God as Father and Jesus as his Son are prepared to go to prove that love.[70]

The rejection of penal substitution is clear. What is not so clear is the meaning of the cross in this new theological perspective. To say that it is a symbol of love is fine but what does that mean? Is this the moral influence theory revisited? Or some other view where the love of God is used to deny or undermine anything that the Scriptures say about sin, judgement, death and hell? Above all, the question must be asked: What is the connection between the 'Christ event' (for Chalke is rightly insistent that cross and resurrection must not be separated) and our salvation?

Penal substitution reaffirmed

In the light of this increasing consensus against penal substitution, then, including many evangelicals, can we maintain penal substitution in 2012 as Packer did in his lecture published in 1974? It is clear that Packer himself believes so. Some thirty years after his original article was published, he contributed an essay to the aforementioned festschrift for Dr Roger Nicole.[71] This essay is not specifically on the issue of penal substitution but it is clear from the article that his view on that subject remains unchanged.

Having restated his commitment to penal substitution, however, he does make three 'caveats against undue narrowness'. In the first place he argues that 'we must not isolate the atonement from God's larger plan and strategy for his world.'[72] His concern here is to ensure that everything is seen in the light of God's eternal purpose. The death and resurrection of Christ is a 'decisive step' but only one step towards the achieving of God's overall plan for humanity and the consummation of all things.

In the second place he says that 'we must not define atonement in single-category terms.'[73] In making this point he is not following those

---

[70] Ibid, pp. 182–3.
[71] 'The Atonement in the Life of the Christian', in *The Glory of the Atonement* (ed. Hill and James), pp. 409–25.
[72] Ibid, p. 415.
[73] Ibid, p. 416.

who say that there are many models, none of which controls the others. He states quite clearly that 'penal substitution (Christ bearing in our place the curse, that is, the retribution that hung over us) is Paul's final and fundamental category for understanding the cross.'[74] He does, however, go on to say, having outlined a number of models and metaphors of atonement, that 'each of these conceptual categories, items already in the technical language of the apostolic age, covers its own distinct area of thought and meaning – its own semantic field, as we say nowadays – and the full range and glory of the atonement only appears when each is delineated in its own terms.'[75]

Perhaps most striking of all is Packer's third caveat, where he places significant emphasis on union with Christ, a theme that was not central to his argument in the earlier paper. He writes:

> we must not treat the atonement as if its direct benefits to believers are the whole of our salvation, for they are not. Benefits that the atonement brings us directly are forgiveness and justification, that is, full cancellation of our demerit and present acceptance of our sinful persons into the covenant fellowship of our holy God; permanent peace with this God and adoption into his family, establishing us as his heirs . . . But the taproot of our entire salvation, and the true NT frame for cataloguing its ingredients, is our union with Christ himself by the Holy Spirit.[76]

Set the atonement in the light of God's overall purpose and plan; make use of every model and metaphor of atonement, albeit under the controlling model of penal substitution; and give proper emphasis to union with Christ. It seems to me that these are significant and valuable caveats, which might well help to reassure some of those who have problems with penal substitution.

Conclusion

It seems to me that Packer's argument in favour of penal substitution, both in its biblical foundations and in its theological development, is fundamentally sound. It must therefore be a matter of some concern that many evangelicals seem to be abandoning a belief in penal sub-

---

[74] Idem.
[75] Idem.
[76] Ibid, pp. 416–17.

stitution in favour of other ways of expressing their understanding of the atonement. At the same time, it must be recognized that there are some complex theological issues at stake in this debate and so we must be willing to do the hard theological work of rethinking such issues as how to solve the apparent inner-Trinitarian conflict required by a doctrine of penal substitution. We must also be prepared to listen to those, like Bruce McCormack, who seek to maintain penal substitution but yet challenge the traditional formulations of the doctrine.

10

The Extent of the Atonement

Introduction

In our studies in the person and work of Christ, we come now to consider the extent of the atonement. Having considered penal substitution as the main Reformed perspective on the nature of the atonement, we must now note that another significant area of debate in Reformed theology concerns the extent of the atonement. Normally when dealing with this subject we are simply asking the question, 'Did Christ die for all human beings or only for the elect?' To approach the subject biblically, however, it is necessary to expand the issue and set it in a wider context. In order to do this, we shall first consider the question of Israel and salvation; second, we shall review the biblical teaching concerning the limited nature of Christ's atoning death; then third, we shall set the debates on this subject in their historical context.

Jesus and Israel

In Romans 11 Paul teaches that, although the gospel has come to the Gentiles, God has not forgotten Israel. Indeed, Israel still plays a significant part in God's plan of salvation. In the previous chapter, Paul had already demonstrated that the way of salvation was simple and accessible to all, whether Jews or Gentiles. He was concerned, however, because although this gospel had been preached, Israel had not accepted it, not through ignorance but through disobedience and rebellion. The question follows: Is their apostasy and rejection by God final or temporary? It is to this question that Paul directs his attention in Romans 11. In verses 1–10 he answers the question with respect to the remnant and in verses 11–24 he answers the question with respect to all Israel. The chapter as a whole falls into three sections. First, there is still a remnant, since not all Israel has rejected God and been rejected by him (1–10). Second, their present rejection is only temporary (11–24). Third, this temporary rejection leads to final salvation (25–36).

In thinking about the extent of the atonement and the corresponding subject of election, this chapter is very important. We are told in the first part of the chapter about the remnant which remained faithful to God. This group is described in verse 5 as 'a remnant chosen by grace.' Israel as a nation did not receive the blessing of God but 'the elect did.' The rest of Israel was 'hardened' (verse 7). The result of this hardening was that Israel became blind and deaf to the truth (verses 8–9).

This is not the end of Israel, as we might expect after these strong words. The truth is that Israel has not stumbled beyond recovery (verse 11) and Paul looks to the day when Israel will be saved (verse 26). In the meantime, 'salvation has come to the Gentiles to make Israel envious' (verse 11). Paul goes so far as to say that he regards his ministry to the Gentiles to be crucial, not least because it might lead Israel to see and understand and believe the gospel (verses 14–15). He goes even further and argues that if the exclusion of Israel has led to salvation for the Gentiles, the inclusion of the Jews in salvation alongside the Gentiles will be like 'life from the dead' (verse 15).

This teaching that God is not finished with Israel and that their final inclusion in salvation is guaranteed is used by Paul to bring humility to the Gentiles. They must not boast about their status in Christ as if it were a trophy they had earned. Their salvation is all of grace and indeed they are nothing more than wild branches grafted on to the native tree, which represents Israel, the chosen people of God (verses 17–24). After all, if branches which don't belong to the tree can be grafted on, how much easier it will be to graft back on the branches which actually belong to the tree, namely, Israel.

In verses 25–29 Paul states his great conclusion regarding the election of Israel and the final salvation in which Israel will participate:

> I do not want you to be ignorant of this mystery, brothers, so that you may not be conceited: Israel has experienced a hardening in part until the full number of the Gentiles has come in. And so all Israel will be saved, as it is written: 'The deliverer will come from Zion; he will turn godlessness away from Jacob. And this is my covenant with them when I take away their sins.' As far as the gospel is concerned, they are enemies on

your account; but as far as election is concerned, they are loved on account of the patriarchs, for God's gifts and his call are irrevocable.

Paul defends this argument by quoting from Isaiah 59:20; Isaiah 27:9; and Jeremiah 31:33. He then notes that the purpose of God for the Jews is intertwined with the purpose of God for the Gentiles (verses 28–30) before concluding with a marvellous doxology in verses 33–34. This doxology concludes not only chapter 11, but the whole section on the relationship between Israel and God's election found in Romans 9 – 11.

In thinking about the extent of the atonement, then, we must not think purely in individualistic terms. There is a corporate dimension both to the atonement and to God's election, and any account of these subjects which does not take seriously the place of Israel in God's plan has singularly failed. Whatever else we might say about the extent of the atonement, we must insist that it has implications for Israel and not only for the Christian church. There is a gathering in, which is yet to come.

Jesus and the elect

Having spoken about Israel, we must now come to the more difficult issue of the relationship between election and the extent of the atonement. We can put the question like this: We believe that Christ died on the cross to save people and deliver them from their sins; but who are these people? Did Christ die for everyone, or for anyone who wanted to claim it, or for a certain group of people?

Paul, in Ephesians 1:1–14, deals with this doctrine of election or predestination. After some preliminary greetings, he says in verse 3 that God has blessed us with every spiritual blessing in Christ. In verses 4 and 5 he goes on to indicate that the first and greatest of these blessings is our election: 'For he chose us in him before the creation of the world to be holy and blameless in his sight. In love he predestined us to be adopted as his sons through Jesus Christ, in accordance with his pleasure and will'. There are three points that we ought to make in relation to this passage. First, Paul uses two expressions: God 'chose us' and God 'predestined us'. These phrases are used interchangeably. To be 'chosen' is to be 'elected' or to be 'predestined'. All of these expressions mean fundamentally the same thing.

The second point is that this predestination was inextricably linked to Jesus Christ. We were chosen 'in him' (meaning 'in Christ'). Then in verse 7, it is 'in him' we have redemption. In verse 11 we read that 'in him' we were chosen. These verses teach us that our salvation from beginning to end is centred in Christ. God chose us to be saved from before the foundation of the world but he did it 'in Christ'. That is why in this passage there is so much emphasis on Christ. We are saved, says Paul, by his blood. Through Christ we receive the 'forgiveness of sins'. We have been predestined to salvation but that predestination is 'in Christ'. We might put it like this: God did not choose us for salvation without also determining the means by which this salvation would be accomplished. That is why thinking about our election leads on naturally to thinking about the atonement.

Third, this election or predestination was for a purpose. He 'chose us in him before the creation of the world to be holy and blameless in his sight.' Also, he chose us 'to be adopted as his sons'. This is very important. God's predestinating grace has two objectives. First, that we should be holy and second, that we should be adopted into the family of God. Following the fall in Genesis 3, our first parents had two problems: they were totally depraved or corrupted because of sin and they were separated from God. As we can see here in Ephesians, God's predestination is designed to deal with both of these problems. Our sinful corruption is dealt with as the Holy Spirit works in us to sanctify us, to make us holy and blameless in Christ, and our separation from God is dealt with when we are adopted into the family of God.

In this chapter of Ephesians, then, we learn something of the nature and purpose of God's electing grace. It is well summed up in verse 11: 'In [Christ] we were also chosen, having been predestined according to the plan of him who works out everything in conformity with the purpose of his will.' Paul is telling us here that God is sovereign and that one aspect of that sovereignty concerns our salvation. That is to say, not only does God work out everything according to his purpose in terms of providence and the events of history but even our very salvation comes about because of God's plan. It is this doctrine of God's unconditional election which helps us to understand the extent of the atonement.

This doctrine of election or predestination is found in many places in Scripture, not just in the letter to the Ephesians. There are references to a company of people spoken of in Scripture as the elect, for example, in 2 Timothy 2:10 and Mark 13:20. These verses speak of the election by God of a people for himself. Sometimes we find just a passing reference to the doctrine. So in a number of places, for example, we find the expression 'the elect' or 'God's elect'. In his second letter to the

Thessalonians, Paul tells them that God chose them to be saved (1:13). Peter, in his first letter, addresses his readers as 'God's elect'.

A more detailed statement is found in Romans 8:28–30:

> And we know that in all things God works for the good of those who love him, who have been called according to his purpose. For those God foreknew he also predestined to be conformed to the likeness of his Son, that he might be the firstborn among many brothers. And those he predestined, he also called; those he called, he also justified; those he justified, he also glorified.

The Reformed churches have taught since the time of the Reformation – and it had been taught much earlier by Augustine and others – that the death of Christ has specific reference to the elect of God. This is also the position taken by many of the confessional documents produced in the post-Reformation period, for example, the *Westminster Confession of Faith*. The elect are all those who will ultimately be in heaven; that is to say, all those both before and after Christ who were, are or will be justified by faith in Christ. In real terms this means the church, or at least the true church.

In Ephesians 5:25 we are told that Christ died for the church. In John 10:15 Jesus says that he lays down his life for the sheep and the verses which follow make it clear that he is speaking of his own sheep. John 11:52 supports and underlines this interpretation where Jesus is said to die for the scattered children of God. In his high priestly prayer in John 17:9 Jesus specifically says that he is not praying for the world, only those whom God the Father had 'given' him. Similarly, in Acts 20:28, we find the affirmation that Christ shed his blood for 'the church': 'Keep watch over yourselves and all the flock of which the Holy Spirit has made you overseers. Be shepherds of the church of God, which he bought with his own blood.'

To support this view that Christ died for the elect, we can consider Mark 10:45: 'For even the Son of Man did not come to be served, but to serve, and to give his life as a ransom for many.' This teaching about the Suffering Servant resonates with what we have already seen in Isaiah 53 but notice what is added here: the Suffering Servant dies for 'the many'. This is similar to saying that Christ died for the 'church' and gave his life for the 'church'.

There are, of course, many Christians who take a different view on this matter. There are some who argue that the death of Christ is like a blank cheque, which anyone with faith and repentance can draw upon.

The problem with this view is that it seems to cast doubt on the sovereign grace of God and to put salvation into our own hands. It becomes a matter of what we do, what we contribute and what we decide and in some sense implies that ultimately it is our decision that saves us. The Reformed doctrine, by contrast, is that Christ died for a specific and definite group of people, the elect, who will certainly and unavoidably be saved. In other words, Christ died to save us, not to make it possible for us to save ourselves. This doctrine is called 'particular redemption' or 'limited atonement'. The idea of a 'limited' atonement seems a terrible concept to many Christians but the fact is that everyone 'limits' the atonement in some way. We either limit its scope (Christ died only for those who will be in heaven) or we limit its effectiveness (he died for everyone but his death is only effective for those who will be in heaven). This 'limiting' is necessary if we are to avoid universalism (Christ died for everyone and everyone will be saved), which we must do because the Bible is clear that there will be a Day of Judgement and that there is a hell. B.B. Warfield puts it this way: 'The things we have to choose between are an atonement of high value, or an atonement of wide extension. The two cannot go together.'[1]

One important point must be made here. Although we may limit the atonement, we do not limit the gospel offer. The Bible teaches that Christ died for the church but it also teaches that we are to preach the gospel to every creature. These two truths must be held together. In early eighteenth-century Scotland there were those who argued that we cannot offer the gospel to anyone unless they were showing 'signs of election' (whatever that might be) and men like Thomas Boston had to stand fast on the importance of the free offer of the gospel. He insisted that Christ died to save sinners and therefore sinners have a warrant to believe on Christ for salvation. We do not know whom God has chosen and so we must preach the gospel to 'every creature without exception'. As we issue the outward call of the gospel, we pray that God will accompany this with the effectual call of his Spirit and so bring men and women and children into his kingdom.

Historical and theological debate

The question of the extent of the atonement became a major battleground in the century following the Reformation. There were two

---

[1] B.B. Warfield, *The Plan of Salvation* (Grand Rapids, MI: Eerdmans, no date), p. 95.

different theories which challenged the earlier Reformed position: Arminianism and Amyraldianism. We shall consider each of these.

Arminianism

Jacobus Arminius (1560–1609) was educated in Switzerland and then served for a time as minister of a church in Amsterdam, during which period he began to question some of the tenets of Calvinism. After various disputes on these matters he left his church and became professor of theology at the University of Leyden.

After his death, the followers of Arminius formulated his teaching in a five-point document entitled *The Remonstrance* and this was published in 1610. Those who held to its teaching were called the 'Remonstrants'. In this document, there were five points of departure from the earlier Calvinism:

1. God's eternal decree was to elect those who would believe in Christ and reject those who would not believe. That is to say, God's election or saving choice is based on God's foreknowledge of who would, or would not, believe of their own free will.
2. The atonement was universal in its extent. Christ died for everyone, not just the elect. Nevertheless, only believers benefit from the death of Christ.
3. The work of the Holy Spirit was necessary in order to bring about regeneration, renewal and sanctification.
4. God's grace is the means by which human beings are saved but this grace can be resisted.
5. It is possible for believers to 'fall from grace' and so to lose their salvation. In other words, it is possible to be a Christian and then, at a later stage, not be a Christian.

This Arminian system of doctrine was condemned at the Synod of Dort in 1618–19. Five counter-theses to the Arminian ones already quoted were put forward and accepted at the synod. More recently, these have been summarised by the mnemonic 'TULIP'. They were:

1. Total Depravity: This is the teaching that every single aspect of human existence has been affected by the fall, including the mind and the emotions as well as nature and will. It does not mean that human beings are as bad as they could be. (Reformed theology has always had a category of 'common grace' by which God

restrains sin and enables even sinners to do good things.)
Nevertheless, the depravity is 'total' and so redemption must deal
with the totality of the problem.

2. Unconditional Election: This is the teaching that human beings are
   chosen for salvation due to the free and sovereign will of God and
   not because of anything they have done to achieve or earn this,
   nor even because of God's foreknowledge of such future decisions
   and works.

3. Limited Atonement: This is the teaching that Christ died specifically and only for those whom God has predestined to salvation.
   His atonement was an act in which he took upon himself the
   penalty for the sins of all those who will one day be in heaven,
   namely, those whom God had decided to save.

4. Irresistible Grace: This is the teaching that all of those individuals
   whom God predestined to salvation will certainly be saved
   because God's call is irrevocable and his saving choice cannot be
   frustrated.

5. Perseverance of the Saints: This is the teaching that can be
   summed up in the expression, 'once saved, always saved'. That is
   to say, it is not possible for the elect to fall from grace, since God
   will not allow this to happen. The thought here is more one of
   'preservation' than 'perseverance'.

Speaking genetically, we might say that Arminianism is a branch of
Reformed theology because it originated with the writing of a
Calvinist professor in a Calvinist institution. For most of its history,
however, Arminianism has been held by those who specifically dis-
tanced themselves from Reformed theology. It is probably the dominant theological position held by most Methodists, Baptists,
Pentecostals and charismatics.

The Reformed rejection of Arminianism centres on two great convictions. First, that all human beings are sinners who are cut off from
God because of sin and are therefore unable to do anything to reverse
or change their condition. Second, that only by the sovereign grace of
God can sinners be lifted out of their sinful condition, have their sins
forgiven and be restored to fellowship with God.

Amyraldianism

Since the Synod of Dort, the mainstream of Reformed theology has
taken the view that the atonement is particular (or limited). That is to

say, Christ's death was for and on behalf of the elect. He did not die for all humanity, although most Reformed theologians would agree that his death was sufficient for all and that it had a certain universal reference, although not in the sense of purchasing salvation for all humanity. This view is enshrined in the later post-Reformation confessional documents, not least the *Westminster Confession of Faith*.

There have always been those within the Reformed tradition who have challenged this account of salvation and have argued that it is a deviation from authentic Calvinism. The contemporary 'Calvin versus Calvinism' debate which has been going on for over thirty years bears witness to this disagreement. Perhaps the most important disagreement within the tradition, however, is between traditional Calvinists and those who take an Amyraldian position. This debate is most hotly contested because, in so many other respects and on so many doctrinal issues, the combatants are in agreement.

Amyraldianism is a system of Christian doctrine which seeks to understand the atonement as being universal in its extent and intention, while at the same time holding to a particularist view of its effect. It is associated with the name of Moise Amyraut (1596–1664) and so-called because of the Latin form of his name (Amyraldus).

In fact, the system can be traced to Amyraut's teacher in the French Protestant Academy of Saumur, John Cameron (1579–1625). Cameron was a Scotsman who taught at Saumur from 1618 to 1621 and had considerable influence on the theological development of Saumur, not least by his impact on several young scholars, of whom Amyraut is the most significant. Amyraut himself taught at Saumur from 1633 until his death in 1664.

The key to understanding Amyraldianism is its notion of a hypothetical universal covenant, which is why Amyraldianism is sometimes called 'hypothetical universalism'. The idea is that the covenant of grace is really two covenants. By this understanding, God made a covenant with all human beings wherein they would be saved on condition of repentance and faith. This was possible at a natural level (the human will was capable of making such a response) but impossible at a moral level (through the inability of human beings to respond because of their sin). This being the case, God made another covenant, this time an unconditional covenant which guarantees the salvation of the elect.

Amyraldianism thus implies a twofold will of God, whereby he wills the salvation of all mankind on condition of faith but wills the salvation of the elect specifically and unconditionally. The theological difficulty of God's will having been frustrated by the fact that not all are saved is met by the argument that God only willed their salvation on the condition of faith. Where an individual has no faith, then God has not willed the salvation of that person.

This theological perspective also implies a twofold intention in the atonement whereby Christ dies in a (hypothetical) universalist sense for all humanity but in a particularist sense for the elect only. It is in this debate on the extent of the atonement that Amyraldianism (or a variant thereof) has maintained its influence to the present day. The debate as to whether or not Calvin taught limited atonement or, if he did not, whether it is a natural and logical outworking of his other doctrines, rumbles on.

Amyraut's intention in developing this theological perspective was a noble one. He wanted to reconcile those of a Reformed persuasion with their Lutheran contemporaries, solve the impasse between those who believed in a universal atonement and those who believed in a limited atonement, and thus unite the Protestant cause. Amyraut had no intention of rejecting the Reformed heritage stemming from Calvin. He believed that the Scriptures did have a universalist as well as a particularist view of the atonement and that both of these had to be expressed in any theology of the atonement. The problem was that Amyraut's solution suited neither the universalists nor the particularists.

Amyraut's views were dealt with at the National Synod of Alençon (1637). Interestingly, although his views were rejected and he was admonished by the Synod, he was not condemned as a heretic.

Saumur became noted for several theological perspectives which differed from the prevailing orthodoxy as represented by the Synod of Dort (1615). As well as Amyraut's views on the nature and extent of the atonement, one of his contemporaries denied verbal inspiration and another taught a view of mediate imputation of Adam's sin to his posterity. All three of these positions were dealt with in the Formula Consensus Helvetica (1675), although particular attention was paid to Amyraldianism which was rejected as being unorthodox.

The famous Amyraldian dictum that Christ died sufficiently for all but efficiently only for the elect was, in fact, a scholastic expression to which even Calvin was prepared to give assent. The Amyraldians, however, used it to mean something which Calvin and the later Reformed theologians rejected, namely, the notion of a universal atonement which was then applied particularistically. This Amyraldian version of the dictum has experienced something of a revival of late through the writings of R.T. Kendall and Alan Clifford. Both have argued that Calvin held to a universal atonement while at the same time affirming a predestination of the elect alone to salvation.

The decision one makes in the Calvinist versus Amyraldian debate depends upon one's view of the order of the decrees of God. Historically, there have been two main positions held within the Reformed community: supralapsarianism and infralapsarianism.

Supralapsarianism is the view which places election and reprobation at the head of the order of decrees (in all that follows, the 'order of decrees' is taken to mean 'logical' and not 'temporal' order). Thus it is taught that the election of some human beings and some angels to eternal life with God preceded the permissive decree of the fall and even the decree of creation. Charles Hodge summarizes this well when he writes:

> According to this view, God in order to manifest his grace and justice selected from creatable men (ie. from men to be created) a certain number to be vessels of mercy and certain others to be vessels of wrath. In the order of thought, election and reprobation precede the purpose to create and to permit the fall. Creation is in order to redemption. God creates some to be saved, and others to be lost.[2]

Karl Barth lists 'Beza, Bucanus, Gomarus, Maccovius, Heidanus and Burmann' as the best known exponents.[3] More recently, supralapsarianism has been advocated by a number of scholars, not least Robert Reymond.[4]

Infralapsarianism is the position held by those who 'conceive that the principle of particularism, in the sense of discrimination, belongs in the sphere of God's soteriological, not in that of his cosmical creation'.[5] In other words, infralapsarianism teaches the order of decrees as being creation, permission for the fall and election to life, hence seeing election as being from the mass of fallen humanity. Both the Synod of Dort and the Westminster Assembly, while not being specific, show clear

---

[2] Charles Hodge, *Systematic Theology* (New York: Scribners, 1874), p. 316.
[3] This was recognized by Barth in his analysis of the problem: *Church Dogmatics* II/ II, p. 127.
[4] Robert L. Reymond, *A New Systematic Theology of the Christian Faith* (Nashville, TN: Nelson, 1998), pp. 488–502.
[5] Warfield, *Plan of Salvation*, p. 88.
[6] Barth, *Church Dogmatics* II/ II, p. 129.

bias towards this position. It is also generally held to be the orthodox view,[6] although attempts to have either position officially condemned have failed.[7]

Amyraldianism (or hypothetical universalism) claims to hold together both the universal reference of the atonement and also its particular application. On the surface, this looks as if it might draw various biblical threads together. Those who hold this position would agree with the infralapsarians that the decree permitting the fall must be prior to the decree of election but between these two is placed the work of Christ, rendering salvation possible for all human beings. Hence there is posited a universal possibility but an elected actuality.

This view has recently been advocated most strongly by Alan C. Clifford, who is persuaded that this is the view held by Calvin himself, although most Calvinists remain unconvinced.[8]

The major problem which opponents raise against both Arminianism and Amyraldianism concerns the justice of God. It is usually expressed in the following way: If Christ died for all human beings, as is claimed, why will all human beings not be saved? Perhaps no-one has more clearly expressed this argument, as well as the many other problems associated with these two theological positions, than the English Puritan theologian, John Owen. He wrote one treatise against Arminianism[9] and another against Amyraldianism (which also dealt with Arminianism).[10]

Owen's argument, particularly in his treatise *The Death of Death in the Death of Christ*, is that if Christ's death paid the penalty for the sins of those who will not be saved then a 'double penalty' is being extracted.[11] That is to say, it is clearly unjust for those who are not saved to pay the penalty for their own sins by enduring eternal

---

[7] See D. Jellema, 'Supralapsarianism', in *The New International Dictionary of the Christian Church* (ed. J.D. Douglas; Exeter: Paternoster, 1974).

[8] Alan C. Clifford, *Atonement and Justification* (Oxford: OUP, 1990); idem, *Calvinus: Authentic Calvinism, A Clarification* (Norwich: Charenton Reformed Publishing, 1996); idem, *Amyraut Affirmed* (Norwich: Charenton Reformed Publishing, 2004).

[9] John Owen, 'A Display of Arminianism', in *The Works of John Owen* (ed. William H. Goold; London: Banner of Truth, 1967), vol. 10, pp. 11–137.

[10] Owen, 'The Death of Death in the Death of Christ', *Works*, vol. 10, pp. 139–428.

[11] For those who might struggle to plough through several hundred pages of Owen, the best short essay on the subject is J.I. Packer's 'Saved by His Precious Blood' which he originally wrote as an introduction to an edition of Owen's *The Death of Death in the Death of Christ* and which can be found in his book *Among God's Giants* (Eastbourne: Kingsway, 1991), pp. 163–95.

punishment in hell, if Christ has already paid the penalty on their behalf. Thus, it is argued, if we are to view Christ's death as being penal and substitutionary, then we must limit the extent of this atonement to those whose sins will be eternally forgiven, which means that we must limit the atonement to the elect.

It seems to me that there is much study still to be undertaken in relation to the extent of the atonement. There also needs to be a degree of humility and openness on the part of those of us who believe in limited atonement. After all, the number of specific references to support limited atonement are few, much of the argument being put together by 'good and necessary consequence' from what the Bible clearly teaches about predestination and other doctrines. There is also the fact that strong references can be brought forward by those who reject the doctrine of limited atonement. For example, in John 4:42 Jesus is described as 'the Saviour of the world.' In 1 Timothy 2:4 Paul says that God our Saviour 'wants all men to be saved and to come to a knowledge of the truth.' Then, in 1 John 2:2, we read that Christ 'is the atoning sacrifice for our sins, and not only for ours but also for the sins of the whole world.' The best Reformed theologians, while not abandoning the doctrine of limited atonement, have recognized the force of these verses and have argued that, at least in some sense, the atonement has universal dimensions. In so doing, they have sought to remember the wider cosmic significance of who Christ is and what he has done.

There has been a tendency to dismiss these matters as debates from a previous century which are either settled or not capable of being settled. Even the most significant popular book on the subject of the cross, by John R.W. Stott, does not have a chapter on the extent of the atonement.[12] There is scope for further work here, which ought to be carried out in engagement with Arminian and Amyraldian scholars, not least because historically both groups have their origins within the Calvinist tradition. In particular, the arguments being presented by the recently reinvigorated Amyraldian position must be tackled and their arguments faced seriously and carefully.

Conclusion

This chapter brings us to the end of our studies in the work of Christ and, having indicated above where further work might usefully be

---

[12] J.R.W. Stott, *The Cross of Christ* (Leicester: IVP, 1986).

done on the extent of the atonement, we ought to pause and note also the need for further work on the nature of the atonement. The doctrine of the atonement is fundamental to our understanding of the Christian faith and we must not be content with a situation where the church remains divided on this matter. Every effort must be made to reach a unified conclusion, albeit firmly based on the teaching of Scripture. Our objective must be to achieve for the doctrine of the work of Christ what has already been achieved for the doctrine of the person of Christ, namely, the near universal agreement of the church. This may seem unrealistic but, like Jesus' prayer in John 17 that the church would be one, it must remain the goal for the theologians of the church. It goes without saying that these further studies need to take place in the context of the church and of ecumenical dialogue, rather than simply in the Academy.

11

Union with Christ

Introduction

We have looked at the various aspects of biblical teaching concerning the doctrines of the person and work of Christ. In considering the person of Christ, we identified him as the Son of God, the Second Person of the Trinity who, at a given point in space and time, took a human nature and became Jesus of Nazareth, while remaining fully and completely God. In considering the work of Christ, we noted that, in our place, he offered himself to the Father as the once-for-all sacrifice for sins, received upon himself the punishment due for those sins and thus paid the penalty, so that sinners might be pardoned and accepted. This leaves us with the critical question as to how all that Christ is and all that Christ has done actually connects with the lives of human beings.

In order to answer this critical question, we shall turn to the doctrine of union with Christ, demonstrating that this is the key to understanding the transformation in human lives as Christ's redemptive work is applied. Before turning to that theme, however, it is necessary to understand the human condition. That is to say, we must establish why it is that human beings need to be united with Christ in order to be in a right relationship with God.

The human condition

Genesis 3 tells the most tragic story in the whole history of the human race. It is no exaggeration to say that the events of Genesis 3 provide the explanation for the sinful condition of human beings and also provide the reason for the coming of Christ. Anyone who does not understand this chapter of Scripture, in all its depth and significance, cannot properly understand the gospel.

In Genesis chapters 1 and 2 we read of God's creation. We are told that everything was very good and that man himself was created upright and without any moral flaw. That is to say, everything was perfect. As we come to Genesis 3, however, that picture changes dramatically. The very first verse of the chapter contains a description of a creature actively working against God and seeking to undermine confidence in him. He is simply described as 'the serpent' but if we go to Revelation 12:9, we find this description: 'that ancient serpent called the devil, or Satan, who leads the whole world astray.' The serpent in Genesis 3, then, is the devil or Satan.

In Job 1:6–7 we learn a little more: 'One day the angels came to present themselves before the LORD, and Satan also came with them. The LORD said to Satan, "Where have you come from?" Satan answered the LORD, "From roaming through the earth and going to and fro in it."' The serpent in Genesis 3, who was Satan, had been one of the angels of God. We are not told much about him but there are several hints in Scripture which suggest that he was perhaps the brightest of all the angels but yet fell from grace through preoccupation with himself and his own glory. Some biblical commentators believe that Isaiah 14:12–15 is referring to what happened to Satan:

> How you have fallen from heaven, O morning star, son of the dawn! You have been cast down to the earth, you who once laid low the nations! You said in your heart, 'I will ascend to heaven; I will raise my throne above the stars of God; I will sit enthroned on the mount of assembly, on the utmost heights of the sacred mountain. I will ascend above the tops of the clouds; I will make myself like the Most High.' But you are brought down to the grave, to the depths of the pit.

Other commentators refer to the words of Jesus in Luke 10:17–19, when seventy-two disciples, whom he had sent out on mission, returned to him. The Scripture says, 'The seventy-two returned with joy and said, "Lord, even the demons submit to us in your name." He replied, "I saw Satan fall like lightning from heaven. I have given you authority to trample on snakes and scorpions and to overcome all the power of the enemy; nothing will harm you."'

From the teaching of Genesis 3, Revelation 12 and Job 1, together with these verses from Isaiah and from Luke, it would seem that the fall of Satan and his angels took place before the fall of mankind in Genesis 3 and indeed was the cause of that subsequent fall. Why Satan and other angels should rebel against God is not explained.

Scripture also tells us that, from the beginning, Satan was a deceiver (2 Corinthians 11:3,14). He is called the 'god of this age' (2 Corinthians 4:4), the 'prince of this world' (John 12:31) and so on. He is the arch-enemy of God and of the kingdom of God.

With that background we can now understand the fall, where our first parents, Adam and Eve, fell into sin and depravity. Satan, under the guise of a serpent, comes to tempt them. Having been placed in the Garden of Eden, they had been told by God that they must not eat from the tree of the knowledge of good and evil located in the middle of the garden. Satan persuaded them otherwise and so they disobeyed God's express command by eating of the forbidden fruit. As we saw when we were considering the nature of Christ's humanity, when God told Adam not to eat fruit from the forbidden tree, he was talking to Adam not as an individual but as representative head of the human race. Hence, when Adam sinned, the judgement fell not only upon him but upon all those whom he represented, namely all humanity. As a result, all human beings are born as sinners and stand under the judgement of God.

The sin of mankind, like that of Satan, consisted in rebellion and pride. There is a principle here which can be put like this: The basis of all sin is to put ourselves, rather than God, at the centre of our thinking, living and decision-making. Until Genesis 3, our first parents were 'God-centred' in that they accepted what God said, believed what God told them, obeyed his commands and lived in fellowship with him. Their whole lives revolved around God and his word to them. That is to say, they lived God-centred lives. In Genesis 3 this changed and they adopted a new way of thinking. They decided that they would listen to God and they would listen to Satan and then they would choose who to believe. That is to say, they put the word of God into the balances and weighed it against the words of Satan. The critical point, however, was the belief that they were capable of making such a choice and reaching such a decision. They had effectively chosen to live self-centred lives, rather than God-centred lives. From this point on, they would decide for themselves what was right or wrong, good or bad, true or false, whereas before they had accepted that it was God's prerogative to make these judgements.

When I studied for a year in the United States in the late 1970s, I had the great privilege to spend an afternoon with Professor Cornelius Van Til of Westminster Theological Seminary. It was through him that I learned this important truth and it changed my whole understanding of the Christian gospel. It is vital that we see the point at issue here.

Many people regard sin simply as human beings making wrong moral choices. It is, in fact, much more radical than that. Sin is the decision to be 'self-centred' (in this technical sense) rather than 'God-centred'. We might put it even more sharply: human beings were designed and created to live in fellowship with God and to live God-centred lives. We were not made with the capacity to determine, independently of God, the nature of truth and morality. It is God who determines what is right and wrong, good and bad, true and false and we must accept these judgements from him. It is human pride and arrogance that affirms our ability and even right to make such judgement calls. In one sense we might say that living self-centred, instead of God-centred, lives makes us less than truly human.

And this affects our knowledge too. No true knowledge can be had of anything unless that knowledge is understood in relation to the Creator, with him at the centre. It is possible to possess a number of facts which in themselves are true but if these facts are not seen in relation to God and the system of thought represented by the Christian faith then they do not constitute real knowledge. We might say that the simplest believer is in possession of more real knowledge than the unbelieving university professor because the small number of facts he does possess are understood accurately, in terms of the Creator and his creation. The brilliant scientist who is an atheist may possess many facts and a great deal of information but he does not truly understand how it all fits together. To that extent he is lacking in knowledge. As we read in Proverbs 1:7, 'the fear of the LORD is the beginning of knowledge.' Cornelius Van Til described the educated atheist as being like someone who had many beads but could not find the ends of the string in order to put them all back together again into a necklace.

If we understand all of this, we can see that Christianity offers a radical critique of the human condition and of all human systems of thought. Human beings are either God-centred or self-centred. That is the true distinction between the believer and the unbeliever. Another way of putting it would be to say that if we are God-centred we are free but if we are self-centred then we are in bondage to Satan. Dr Sinclair Ferguson puts it like this: 'The ultimate tragedy of man's self-understanding is that he believes himself to be free, has all the feelings of a free agent, but does not realise that he is a slave to sin and serves the will of Satan.'

If we return to Genesis 3, we can see that the transition of Adam and Eve from their God-centred to their self-centred position had immediate and dramatic consequences. They became aware of their guilt and experienced immediate separation from God with whom they had previously been intimate and with whom they had shared daily fellowship. In verse 8 we are told that 'they hid from the LORD God'. As a result of their sin, they were banished from the garden and they received the sentence for their disobedience: toil, sorrow and death for humanity and a blight upon the created order.

From this point on human beings are perverted creatures. They have ceased to be truly human and the image of God within them has been defaced and damaged. Speaking of Adam and Eve, the *Westminster Confession of Faith* puts it like this: 'They being the root of all mankind, the guilt of this sin was imputed, and the same death in sin and corrupted nature conveyed to all their posterity, descending from them by ordinary generation.' Paul gave a graphic account of this human condition in Ephesians 2:1–3, as he spoke of what the Christians in Ephesus had been and what they had become:

> As for you, you were dead in your transgressions and sins, in which you used to live when you followed the ways of this world and of the ruler of the kingdom of the air, the spirit who is now at work in those who are disobedient. All of us also lived among them at one time, gratifying the cravings of our sinful nature and following its desires and thoughts. Like the rest, we were by nature objects of wrath.

It is vital that we understand this doctrine of sin if we are to see the ruin and misery from which Christ has redeemed us. Having identified the origins of human sin and the tragic reality of the human condition, we can see clearly the contrast between sin and salvation. Over against the darkness of Genesis 3, the light of the glory of Christ shines brightly. With that background we can now turn to the way in which redemption is applied to human beings.

Effectual calling

The beginning of the process whereby what Christ has accomplished is applied to human beings has been named 'effectual calling'. In Romans 8:28–30 Paul describes the process leading to the glorification of believers in heaven:

> And we know that in all things God works for the good of those who love him, who have been called according to his purpose. For those

> God foreknew he also predestined to be conformed to the likeness of
> his Son, that he might be the firstborn among many brothers. And those
> he predestined, he also called; those he called, he also justified; those he
> justified, he also glorified.

In order to understand the identity of those 'who have been called
according to his purpose' we must ask what 'called' means in these
verses.

In this passage, there is no reason to believe that the number of people involved at each stage in this process is different. It does not say
that 'some' of those who were predestined were called and 'some' of
those who were called were justified and 'some' of those who were
justified were glorified. The clear sense of the passage is that 'all'
those who were predestined will be glorified. That being the case, we
can now ask what 'called' means here. It cannot mean the outward
call of the gospel, since many of those who are called in this outward
way, perhaps through being present in church when the gospel is
preached, do not become Christians. In the passage, 'all' who are
called go on to be justified and glorified. This means that the 'call'
described in this passage must be taken to be an 'effectual call' rather
than simply the outward call issued every time the gospel is
preached. We should also note that, as God the Father is the agent of
predestination, so also he is the agent in effectual calling: 'those
whom he predestined, he also called'. The specific result of this effectual call is that we are brought into union with Christ.

Union with Christ

It is at this point we must speak about the work of the Holy Spirit.
There is, after all, a very obvious problem. Given the human condition as described above, how can sinners, who are spiritually dead
and separated from God, respond to the summons contained in this
effectual call? The answer is that they are enabled to do so by the Holy
Spirit. When the outward call of the gospel is issued, the Holy Spirit
grants the gift of faith to those sinners who have been chosen 'in
Christ'. In the exercise of this faith, sinners are united to Christ and so
are enabled to respond to the call. As Paul says in Romans 10:17, 'faith
comes from hearing the message, and the message is heard through
the word of Christ.' Thus the outward call becomes an 'effectual call'
through the gift of faith, by which the sinner is brought into union

with Christ. Having been united with Christ, every benefit and blessing which sinners receive flows from that relationship. Thereafter,
every aspect of our salvation is understood in relation to the fact that
we have been united with Christ.

The various acts and processes which constitute redemption have
not always been viewed in their proper relation to the doctrine of
union with Christ. In the history of Christian theology, many debates
have taken place concerning the 'order of salvation' and this has
raised some difficult questions, not least the way in which faith, union
with Christ, regeneration, justification, adoption, repentance and
sanctification relate to one another. There has been a tendency in
Reformed theology to see the doctrines relating to salvation as an
'order of salvation' and the impression is often given that they are like
a series of dominoes, so laid out that when one falls, each of the others follow in turn. On this account, effectual calling is followed by
regeneration, which is followed by justification, which is followed by
sanctification and so on. Now there is some merit in laying out these
various doctrines side by side, in order to examine each one individually, but the more important truth is that each of these describes
something which happens to us when we are united to Christ. Our
justification is 'in Christ', our sanctification is 'in Christ' and every
gift, blessing and benefit we receive from God is 'in Christ'.

This also helps us to avoid another problem. In one sense, we must
understand the application of the death of Christ to the lives of sinners in 'forensic' terms, as a transaction between the Father and the
Son in which certain benefits are obtained and subsequently passed
on to us by imputation. Nevertheless, if we view the application of
redemption purely in forensic terms, we miss something very important. Indeed, some expressions of this forensic view have led to the
work of Christ being regarded as something entirely detached and
external. It is something that is done 'for us' rather than 'in us'. The
relation between the forensic (the redemption purchased for us by
Christ) and the ontological (our union with Christ) must be kept in
balance. Some scholars have so emphasized union with Christ that
the imputation of the righteousness of Christ appears to play no part
in their thinking. Others have so emphasized the forensic aspect of
salvation that it seems to be separated from our life in Christ. Both are
essential.

This teaching on union with Christ as the means by which redemption is applied is central to the teaching of Scripture. The phrase 'in
Christ' appears almost 100 times in the New Testament and there are

many references to 'in the Lord' and 'with Christ' which have a similar meaning. John Murray ably demonstrates from Scripture that
every aspect of our salvation is viewed from the perspective of our
union with Christ. He points out that God chose us 'in Christ' before
the foundation of the world (Ephesians 1:4), that we are united with
Christ in his death and resurrection (Romans 6:2–11), that Christian
life and behaviour are viewed 'in Christ' (1 Corinthians 6:15–17) and
that we die 'in Christ' (1 Thessalonians 4:14–16).[1]

The most significant passage for an understanding of the doctrine
of union with Christ is undoubtedly Romans 6. In order to fully
appreciate the doctrine of union with Christ as Paul expounds it in
that chapter, we need to understand the flow of his argument. In
3:21–31, having demonstrated earlier that no-one can be justified
before God by obedience to law (written or unwritten), Paul says that
only by faith in Jesus Christ can we be in a right relationship with
God. In chapter 4 he shows that Abraham was justified by faith, in
order to answer the Jews who thought that Abraham was saved by
works of obedience. Then in 5:1–11 he notes that our justification is
only possible because of the death and resurrection of Jesus Christ. At
this point in the argument, in 5:12–21, Paul teaches us that every
human being is either in Adam or in Christ. The one way leads to
death and the other way leads to life. This is critical to the whole argument and indeed critical to our understanding of the gospel. We saw
in earlier chapters that Adam was the 'representative' head of the
human race, such that when he sinned this impacted on all humanity. In Romans 5:12–21 we see the other side of this, namely, that those
who are in union with Christ, the new 'representative' head, will be
delivered from sin and will be saved. As Paul says in 1 Corinthians
15:22, all who are in Adam will die and all who are in Christ will be
made alive.

Having thus noted the significance of union with Christ in the second half of chapter 5, Paul expounds the meaning and significance of
this union in chapter 6, not least in its moral and spiritual dimensions.
Here we see the implications of union with Christ for the life of the
believer. Paul begins Romans 6:1 with a strong statement: 'What shall
we say, then? Shall we go on sinning, so that grace may increase?'
Now this is a natural response to Paul's theology if not examined
carefully. Paul is responding to an objector who, having read 5:20,

---

[1] John Murray, *Redemption Accomplished and Applied* (Grand Rapids, MI: Eerdmans,
1955), pp. 162–3.

responds by saying, 'If God's grace so increases when we sin, then why not sin and let it so increase?' In other words, if God is going to forgive all of our sins because we have been justified by faith, why shouldn't we just carry on sinning? As someone with no understanding of the gospel might put it, 'I like sinning and God likes forgiving; it's the perfect arrangement!'

This, of course, can never be right thinking. Having posed the question in verse 1, in verse 2 Paul declares the objection to be unfounded and is apparently amazed at its absurdity. He explains in verses 3–4 that such an attitude is impossible because we have died to sin, been made alive in Christ and so we now live a new life. This is critical to Paul's argument because it underlines the fact that God does not simply forgive us; he also unites us with Christ and transforms us. If God simply wiped the slate clean of our sins but left us in our fallen, sinful condition, then very soon we would be in as bad a condition as before. In fact, however, he enables us to die to one way of life and rise to another and this is symbolized in baptism.

With all of that by way of introduction, Paul now expounds in more depth the doctrine of union with Christ. This is what he says in verses 5–11:

> If we have been united with him like this in his death, we will certainly also be united with him in his resurrection. For we know that our old self was crucified with him so that the body of sin might be done away with, that we should no longer be slaves to sin – because anyone who has died has been freed from sin. Now if we died with Christ, we believe that we will also live with him. For we know that since Christ was raised from the dead, he cannot die again; death no longer has mastery over him. The death he died, he died to sin once for all; but the life he lives, he lives to God.

The key to understanding this transformation is our union with Christ. By faith we enter into a spiritual union with Christ and it is in this union with Christ that all of the blessings of salvation come to us. No wonder, then, that Paul can say in these verses that it is impossible for anyone to share the benefits of Christ's death without sharing in his life also. Paul is teaching us that, in some mysterious way, we share spiritually in the life of the risen Christ. The consequence of this is that, just as Christ died once for all to pay the penalty for sin, so our separation from sin is once for all. There is all the difference in the world between this and legalism. Some Christians in Paul's day (and some in our day) believed that obedience to the law was a condition of salvation. They also believed that emphasizing obedience to the law was the way to ensure that people lived godly lives. Paul places all his emphasis on the fact that believers have been united to Christ in his death and in his resurrection and so the transformation which takes place in the life of the believer is brought about by spiritual union with Christ, rather than by our obedience to the written code.

Our response to God's grace is to live out this new life in spiritual union with Christ. Paul, as usual, is very practical and down to earth, as we see from verses 11–14:

> In the same way, count yourselves dead to sin but alive to God in Christ Jesus. Therefore do not let sin reign in your mortal body so that you obey its evil desires. Do not offer the parts of your body to sin, as instruments of wickedness, but rather offer yourselves to God, as those who have been brought from death to life; and offer the parts of your body to him as instruments of righteousness. For sin shall not be your master, because you are not under law, but under grace.

Practical application

This doctrine of union with Christ is profoundly practical and pastoral because it underlines the fact that the Christian life is not just about living *for* Christ; it is also about living *in* Christ. Let me explain this with a personal illustration. When I became a Christian, I was told to read my Bible every day, to pray every day, to take opportunities to witness for Christ and to go to church. I was also told that there are some things a Christian should do and some things a Christian should not do. This amounted to a set of rules and guidelines. Now most of that was useful and important but there was one major flaw in this guidance: it was all about me and the things I had to do and the things I must not do. The problem is that if you try to live the Christian life in this way, you are constantly depending on your own resources. Then, if you feel that your Christian life is not developing as it should, you say to yourself: I must read my Bible more, I must pray more, I must get to church more, or whatever. In other words, you look to the things that you can do, whereas the real way to deepen and develop our Christian lives is to focus on what Christ has done and upon our relationship with him.

I don't remember anyone telling me that the Christian life is about being united with Christ and so being caught up into the very life of God, drawing all our life and strength from him. That would have helped enormously in the daily life of faith and in the struggle against temptation and sin. Instead, I felt constantly thrown back on my own (limited and frail) resources. Once we discover the glorious truth of our union with Christ, however, everything is transformed. When Paul wanted to minister to churches where there were problems, he never pointed people to their own resources but always directed them to Christ and to their identity in him. For example, in Philippians 2:1 he reminds the Philippians that they are 'united with Christ'. This surely is the key to spiritual life and growth. That is why Paul can say in 2 Corinthians 5:17, 'Therefore, if anyone is in Christ, he is a new creation; the old has gone, the new has come!' In other words, both the beginning and the development of our Christian lives have to do with being 'in Christ', being spiritually united to him. This means that, when we face problems in our Christian lives, we should not focus on what we can do (although sometimes there are things we ought to do) but rather focus on Christ and our union with him. Paul expresses this very well in Colossians 3:1–4: 'Since, then, you have been raised with Christ, set your hearts on things above, where Christ is seated at the right hand of God. Set your minds on things above, not on earthly things. For you died, and your life is now hidden with Christ in God. When Christ, who is your life, appears, then you also will appear with him in glory.'

Some have misconstrued these verses from Colossians 3 as suggesting that believers are actually absorbed into the being of God. Others have similarly interpreted the phrase 'participate in the divine nature' in 2 Peter 1:4. The fundamental distinction between the Creator and the creature is so vital that we cannot contemplate such an interpretation. We never become God or even part of God; we always remain creatures, albeit we are caught up into union with God through our union with the Son of God. Rather, we must interpret these verses as speaking about our union with Christ.[2]

---

[2] See my article 'Colossians 3: Deification, Theosis, Participation, or Union with Christ?', in *Theological Commentary: Evangelical Perspectives* (ed. R. Michael Allen; London: T&T Clark, 2011), pp. 154–71.

Conclusion

Many books have been written about Jesus Christ. Some of them have sought to uncover the 'real Jesus' while others have been content to analyze his moral teaching. Some have been very detached and academic in nature, others popular and biographical. What we have tried to do in this chapter is highlight the fact that knowledge regarding the person and work of Christ is not enough. Only when we enter into union with Christ will his person become a living reality to us and his work of redemption a personal benefit.

12

The Uniqueness of Christ

Introduction

In this book we have tried to lay out the biblical teaching on the person and work of Christ, together with an explanation of the historical process which led to the church reaching theological conclusions, based on this biblical teaching. In writing about Jesus Christ, however, we are not simply writing the biography of a famous man; rather we are describing the dramatic entry of the Son of God into our world. This being the case, a response is necessary and so we turned to the doctrine of union with Christ, being the means by which we enter into the benefits of the redemption which Christ obtained and into a permanent relationship with the living God.

In this final chapter, there is one further important point to be made, namely, that Jesus Christ is the only way provided for human beings to come to God the Father and to be instated in a relationship with him. The argument of this book is not that union with Christ is one way to be right with God, recognizing that other people find different ways. We are saying emphatically that Jesus Christ is the only way to God. This may sound arrogant but if we are Christians we cannot avoid the clear teaching of Scripture regarding the identity of Jesus Christ and the claims of Jesus Christ. As to his identity, God has revealed to us in Scripture that Jesus Christ is the Son of God, the full and final revelation of God. He is not simply a prophet or messenger, who might then be compared and contrasted with other so-called prophets and messengers, such as those espoused by other religions. Jesus Christ is the very incarnation of the living God, in whom all the fulness of the godhead lives in bodily form. As to his claims, we need go no further than John 14:6, where Jesus said, 'I am the way and the truth and the life. No-one comes to the Father except through me.'

The uniqueness of Christ has been axiomatic in Christian theology through most of the past two millennia. It has been regarded as a fundamental, non-negotiable doctrine. The mainstream churches, whether Orthodox, Roman Catholic or Protestant, have all affirmed both his humanity and his divinity and have upheld the statements about him in the creeds and councils of the early church. That consensus is now under threat. Following hard upon the heels of theological liberalism (and as a stepchild of liberalism) has come religious pluralism, which denies the uniqueness of Christ.

Pluralism has offered various proposals but these centre on the conviction that there are many ways to God (if there is a God) of which Jesus of Nazareth is but one. This conviction is a fairly recent phenomenon and is only now beginning to have effect in the churches. It involves a belief that all religions are really expressions of the same human search for ultimate reality. It also usually involves a commitment to bringing the religions together for inter-faith worship, on the grounds that we are all worshipping the same god in different ways. This has become an accepted theological position in many Christian denominations.

There was, nevertheless, a man who lived on this earth approximately two thousand years ago who made certain remarkable claims for himself. These claims were substantiated by certain miracles, not least his resurrection from the dead, reported by a number of eyewitnesses. This man also said that only by believing in him was salvation possible, and only by believing in him would people receive eternal life. What are we to make of him? It is this matter of the uniqueness of Jesus Christ which will be the focus of this final chapter. As we shall see, there are philosophical, political and religious arguments which are presented against any claim to the uniqueness of Christ. Having looked at some of these, we shall then turn to look at two examples in the New Testament of how the apostles viewed these matters, before coming to some conclusions.

Philosophical arguments

The worldview which was adopted by the men and women of the Enlightenment is called 'modernism'. It was optimistic about the ability of human beings to discover all truth by means of unaided reason. It was also optimistic about the power of human beings (without any need for God) to create the perfect society. Today, however, modernism is dead and buried. The enthronement of reason, accompanied by the rejection of any belief in revelation from God and the teaching of the church, has been demonstrated to have been a failure. Belief in human autonomy and the idea of progress towards the perfect society has been destroyed by two world wars within a generation, the mass murder of six million Jews in Hitler's death camps, the ethnic cleansing in the Balkans in the 1990s and similar events in Africa and the Middle East.

The result of the death of modernism is 'postmodernism', which admits that modernism is dead, recognizes that reason alone can get us nowhere, is pessimistic and disillusioned and does not believe any longer in the concept of truth. Everything is relative and therefore what is true for you may not be true for me. Every opinion is as valuable as any other opinion and there are no criteria for determining what is true and what is false, what is good and what is bad, what is right and what is wrong. In fact, even these very ideas of true and false, good and bad, right and wrong, have been abandoned by many postmodernists because they imply that we are able to make judgements.

From this starting point we can never claim anything to be true or authoritative or final. At best we can offer an opinion, or a position which might be a starting point for discussion. Everything becomes relative and, in the end, this destroys the very fabric of rational thought and discussion. In particular, it destroys Christianity. After all, when we as Christians speak of Christ we do not believe that we are offering an opinion, or contributing to a debate; we believe that we are speaking of God incarnate who has final authority because of who he is.

When I was a theological student at Aberdeen University in the early 1970s, there were often interesting and strongly argued debates among the students, mainly on religion and politics! In the debates about religion, particularly in the halls of residence, there was an interesting mix of views: from Christians, Muslims, atheists, agnostics and so on. There was, however, an agreed understanding of the nature of this debate. If it could be proven that Jesus was the Son of God, then everyone would have to accept this. If it could be proven that there was no God, everyone would have to accept this. If Islam could be proven to be God's final word to humanity, then Christians would have to accept this. In other words, we recognized that our competing truth claims stood in contradiction to each other and therefore could not all be true. Today in the average university if you say to someone that you are a Christian, they might well say, 'It's great if that works for you; I'm a Buddhist and that works for me.' There is, among many students, no concept of competing truth claims, no suggestion that if Christianity be true then other religions must, at least in some senses, be false. Truth is no longer the significant issue; rather it is a pragmatic sense of 'what works for me'.

This leaves the Christian apologist (defender of the faith) with a battle on two fronts. A number of people (albeit a decreasing number) deny the claim that Jesus is God because they are modernists. They believe in the final power of their own autonomous reason and, since they can't prove it rationally, then it can't be true. An increasing number of people deny the claim that Jesus is God because they are postmodernists. They don't believe that there is such a thing as truth in the first place.

Political arguments

The challenge to the uniqueness of Christ has also begun to come from politicians. It has now become politically correct in our society to affirm pluralism. In effect, we are being asked to put Christianity alongside other religions as if it were just one option among many. We are being asked to put Jesus Christ alongside the leaders of the world's religions, as just another religious leader. This can sound very reasonable and very tolerant, until we remember that Jesus Christ did not claim to be one way to God among many; he claimed to be God incarnate. If he was, then we must worship him alone and if he wasn't, then Christianity has no reason for existence. Yet the challenge facing Christians on this matter is very real.

I recall the argument which went on at the time of the establishment of the new Scottish parliament, concerning whether or not there would be daily prayer in the parliament. In the initial phase of discussion, it was decided that there would not be prayer. Later, it was argued that there *should* be prayer but that this should not be Christian prayer; rather it should be prayers from all the religions. This argument was pressed, despite the fact that the Church of Scotland was established by numerous Acts of Parliament and holds a unique legal position in the life of the nation. This was an early indication that the new parliament, though very strong on the history of Scotland as a formerly independent nation, was largely ignorant and uncaring with respect to the legal, historical and religious place of the Church of Scotland in the life of the nation.

In both the United Kingdom parliament and the Scottish parliament we have seen progressively the use of 'equality laws' to marginalize Christians. There have been instances, well documented by the Christian Institute, where Christians have been unable to exercise their Christian beliefs because of these so-called 'equality laws'. We might think of the employee who was forbidden from wearing a cross round her neck at work, or the couple who run a bed-and-breakfast establishment and who were taken to court (and lost on appeal), accused of discrimination because they refused to allow a homosexual couple to share a bed in their house. The Roman Catholic Church was forced to withdraw from adoption services because its officials refused to place children with homosexual couples.

In all of these cases and many more, the argument has been that the parliaments and the courts must be 'fair' to people of every religion, ethnic background and sexual orientation. What is not clear is how this is 'fair' to those who hold orthodox Christian beliefs. The problem is that 'equality legislation', which is intended to support the creation of a multi-faith society and an inclusive society, actually militates against the exclusivity of the claims about Jesus Christ. In effect, there is an increasing tendency to make exclusive claims illegal under equality legislation. More recently, this has surfaced in what are called 'hate crimes' where the key issue is freedom of speech. After all, what might be simple Christian teaching might be 'offensive' to someone. Street preachers who have declared the uniqueness of Christ and suggested that other religions are false have been interviewed by the police.

This whole area is the place where the battle lines are increasingly being drawn and will almost inevitably be the place where Christians come into conflict with the prevailing consensus of opinion within our society. It is already considered to be arrogant to suggest that Jesus Christ is the only way to God. It could yet become illegal. One might have expected laws of this nature to be passed in Islamic countries or atheistic dictatorships but in the United Kingdom? The coronation oath identifies the monarch as 'Defender of the Faith', clearly meaning the Protestant faith since Roman Catholics are excluded from office. The oath also requires the monarch to protect the status of the Church of England and the Church of Scotland. Indeed, the monarch is the supreme governor of the Church of England. This religious establishment is seen at many levels of government and public life in both England and Scotland. It cannot be changed except by Act of Parliament. Despite this, there has been growing concern among church leaders, in recent years, about the changing consensus within society on these matters and the danger that presents to the freedom of Christians and to the place of religion in national life.

In 2006 the Evangelical Alliance called upon Prince Charles to affirm that, when he becomes king, he will take the coronation oath as it stands, given that he famously said he would prefer to be 'defender of faiths' rather than 'Defender of the Faith'. In the same year, it was reported in the *Telegraph* that the Church of England had prepared a report in which it objected to Britain being called a multicultural society, arguing that, in fact, it is a Christian country. The authors of the report pointed out that in the last census 72 per cent of people said that they were Christian and only 3 per cent were Muslim. It said that 'the attempt to make minority "faith" communities more integrated has backfired, leaving society "more separated than ever before"' and went on to claim that 'divisions between communities have been deepened by the Government's "schizophrenic" approach to tackling multiculturalism. While trying to encourage interfaith relations, it has actually given "privileged attention" to the Islamic faith and Muslim communities.'[1]

The Evangelical Alliance and the Church of England were surely right to raise these concerns, given the legal status of Christianity as the established religion of the country. The situation has grown steadily more critical since 2006. In 2012 some atheists went to the High Court and had it declared illegal for councils in England and Wales to begin their meetings with prayers! At the same time, both the United Kingdom parliament and the Scottish parliament have issued consultation documents arguing for a change in the law to create 'homosexual marriage'. Cardinal Keith O'Brien in March 2012 issued a fierce condemnation of this and all of the main churches in Scotland submitted documents to the parliament's consultation arguing for the retention of traditional definitions of marriage.

It is important to step back from these controversies and to ask how we arrived at this situation. I recall hearing Sir Frederick Catherwood, former vice-president of the European parliament, argue on one occasion that Britain could become a totalitarian state within a relatively short time. I was astonished at this until he spelled out his most compelling argument. Essentially, he said that where there was no agreed moral and spiritual basis for a society, then governments themselves would decide what was good or bad, true or false, right or wrong.

---

[1] http://www.telegraph.co.uk/news/uknews/1530874/Drive-for-multi-faith-Britain-deepens-rifts-says-Church.html (accessed 27 March 2012).

This would have the added consequence that there would then be no publicly recognized standard against which politicians and the parliaments could be judged.

Not for the first time, Catherwood has proved prophetic. Both the prime minister of the United Kingdom parliament and the first minister of the Scottish parliament seem to believe that they have a right to define marriage, irrespective of the fact that marriage is part of the very fabric of human society as created by God and as such is not a matter for meddling politicians. In addition, we see parliaments legislating for morality on other matters. In the debates on abortion, on homosexuality, on cloning and on other key ethical issues today, the decisions are made largely on the basis of scientific possibilities and majority vote. The Christian faith having been relegated to the margins of society, morality has been weakened and compromised.

This move towards a secular society also has some sinister dimensions. Ever since the Enlightenment of the eighteenth century, there has been a process of secularization taking place which has affected most nations, especially in the western world. This process seeks to remove any trace of religion, faith or the supernatural from institutions and organizations and certainly from public life. At its heart, secularism is a movement which believes that human autonomy and the power of reason are the two controlling features of intellectual life. In other words, human beings are in control and not God. There was a chilling example of this recently in the *Herald* newspaper.[2] The article in question was an abridgement of a section of a book entitled *The Meaning of the 21st Century* by James Martin of Oxford University. In it we read this: 'Evolution has been in nature's hands. Now, suddenly, it is largely in human hands. This transfer of power is by far the largest change to occur since the first single-cell life appeared. Its consequences will be enormous. Now that we are in charge, we need to learn the rules and use our scientific know-how as responsibly as possible.' Notice that phrase: 'now that "we" are in charge'. This kind of thinking is the end product of secularization. It only takes a few determined people with a secular agenda to bring pressure on decision-makers.

There are even those who argue that there should be no involvement of religion at all in public life. Some time ago I was listening to the radio and heard a woman making sarcastic and derogatory remarks about the prime minister because he had dared to mention

---

[2] *The Herald*, 'Comment' column, Friday 6 October 2006, p. 1

his faith and his relationship with God. 'We like our religion to be kept private in this country,' the woman trumpeted and went on to make it very clear that politicians (and everyone else) should keep their religious views to themselves and should not bring them into public life. This is a fairly common opinion today, one which regards religion as a matter of personal devotion, a private communion between an individual and God. Those who take this view argue that one's faith should never be spoken of publicly, since it has no bearing on public issues and will in any case probably cause embarrassment!

Despite its popularity, this view of religion is of relatively recent origin. For almost the entire history of the nation, Christianity has been a very public religion and one which rightly expected to be heard and heeded in the corridors of power. The United Kingdom was regarded as a Christian country; Christian convictions provided the basis for much of our law and also determined the accepted norms of our society. As a minister of the Church of Scotland I can remember the day, not very long ago, when the views of the Church of Scotland would be properly and fully reported in the broadsheet newspapers, not least during the week of the General Assembly when several pages would be devoted to the Kirk each day. That was a time when politicians, the media, captains of industry and the general public would sit up and take notice of what the Kirk said, and not simply when the matter under discussion was controversial.

Now this is not simply a nostalgic look back to the days when the church was considered to be important; there is an important theological principle at stake here. Christianity can never be reduced to a private, mystical relationship between the individual and God because the gospel calls us to have a prophetic ministry, to call the nations to account when they disobey God's law and turn their backs on truth and justice and righteousness. Our forefathers understood that part of the duty of the church was to be firmly rooted in the public square and to speak prophetically about the state of the nation. The bottom line is that we cannot determine truth and morality by majority vote, as if human beings had the right to define these things. There must be a theological basis for all morality and ethics and that can only be found in the self-revelation of God.

As we can surely see, the determination on the part of many (especially some of our leading politicians) to reject the uniqueness of Christ has not only had religious consequences for the churches and interfered with the freedoms of individual Christians; it has actually been deeply damaging to the whole structure of our society.

Religious arguments

We have seen the philosophical and political arguments against the uniqueness of Christ and we might well have expected this. What is most striking (and astonishing) is that there are many within the Christian churches who also reject the uniqueness of Christ. It is not uncommon to find church leaders and theologians preaching this message. They tell us that we must replace evangelism with dialogue and that we have no right to try and persuade people of a different religion to become Christians. If some of today's church leaders had been present in Athens with Paul, they would probably have advised him to get the city authorities to add an idol to Jesus alongside all the other idols! As a minister of the Church of Scotland I have seen numerous examples of this trend towards a denial of the uniqueness of Christ. Perhaps four examples will help to illustrate the problem.

I recall attending a Presbytery meeting some years ago when an evangelical convenor of a major committee put forward the proposal that we should appoint an evangelist to work among Muslims, in order to share the good news about Jesus Christ. This was opposed by some members of the presbytery, who insisted that what we need today is not mission but dialogue, not evangelism but mutual co-operation and understanding. These members of Presbytery were of the view that we have no right to impose our beliefs on those people of another faith.

On another occasion, when a minister, who was a member of Presbytery, completed his year as moderator of the General Assembly of the Church of Scotland, he was asked by Presbytery to give an account of his year in office. He said that the highlights of his year were two interfaith services, in which he had taken part, when Muslims, Jews and Christians came together to worship God, each using their own prayers and their own holy books. He clearly believed that this was the way forward for the church.

The third example was when a minister of the Church of Scotland said that salvation was like a journey to the top of a mountain. We Christians are going up from our side, the Jews, Muslims, Hindus, Buddhists and others are going up from other sides and we'll all meet at the top! Clearly this minister believed that there are many ways to God, of which Christianity was just one among others. The fact that this was a denial of the uniqueness of Christ, and was contrary both to Scripture and to the church's Confession of Faith, seemed to make no difference.

The fourth example comes from the Presbytery of Aberdeen. It was discovered that one congregation was permitting its building to be used for Hindu worship. The matter was brought to the presbytery, which decided that no action should be taken against the congregation in question. Clearly there were many in that presbytery who had no problems at all with this situation. The Church of Scotland has never affirmed pluralism but these examples demonstrate, at the very least, that there is a body of opinion within the church which would gladly do so. From conversations and reading, it is clear that every major denomination has a similar tendency within its membership and ministry.

Biblical response

Sometimes people argue that a multi-faith society is a new phenomenon and therefore Christianity must adapt its theology in order to cope with this changed circumstance. The truth is, of course, that Christianity was born into a multi-faith society and the first Christians lived their lives in the context of that reality. It is instructive to ask, therefore, how they coped with this situation. Did they water down their views on the uniqueness of Christ in the face of a multi-faith society? Or did they stand firm in their beliefs? In order to answer this question, we are going to consider two incidents: when Peter and John were taken before the Sanhedrin in Acts 4 and when Paul visited Athens in Acts 17.

Peter and John

Acts 4:1–22 tells the story of Peter and John before the Sanhedrin. The background to this story is found in chapter 3 of the Acts of the Apostles where God had used Peter to heal a crippled beggar outside the Temple. He healed him in the name of Jesus Christ and immediately began to speak to the crowd about Jesus Christ. Shortly afterwards, Peter and John are arrested by the temple guards and thrown into prison. The next day they were taken before the Sanhedrin. The question which they were asked is very important: 'By what power or what name did you do this?' Notice, there is no argument about the facts. The man was healed; everyone could see that. Peter's response is recorded for us in verses 8–12, the crucial sentence being found in verse 12. Speaking of Jesus Christ, Peter says, 'Salvation is found in no-one else, for there is no other name under heaven given to men by which we must be saved.' There can be no doubt about what Peter is saying here. He is speaking of the uniqueness of Christ. He is saying that salvation is to be found only in Christ. This is similar to Paul's assertion, in 1 Timothy 2:5, that there is only one Mediator between God and humanity, the man Jesus Christ.

Peter's answer to the question posed by the Sanhedrin threw them into a measure of confusion. As we read in Acts 4:13–14, 'When they saw the courage of Peter and John and realised that they were unschooled, ordinary men, they were astonished and they took note that these men had been with Jesus. But since they could see the man who had been healed standing there with them, there was nothing they could say.' After some consideration, however, the Sanhedrin reached a decision. Peter and John were commanded 'not to speak or teach at all in the name of Jesus' (verse 18). This, of course, was a command which Peter and John simply could not and would not accept. They had a burning passion for the gospel and so they stated plainly that they must obey God rather than the Sanhedrin (verse 19).

This is the only time in the New Testament when Christians deliberately disobey the governing authorities. Paul makes it clear, especially in Romans 13, that Christians are to be good citizens, obedient to the state. He says elsewhere that we are to pay our taxes and pray for those who rule over us, yet here is an exception. If the state commands us to do something which requires us to deny the uniqueness of Christ, or tries to silence our right to speak of Christ, then we have not only a right but a duty to disobey.

Paul in Athens

The second incident worth considering, in relation to the way in which the early Christians maintained their faith in a multicultural and multi-religious society, is Paul's visit to Athens, recorded in Acts 17. Athens was a great city in the ancient world, a city of high culture, of great architectural beauty, the home of fine sculptors, writers and orators. In particular it was a city famous for its philosophers and thinkers. Perhaps the best description of the city is given in verse 21 of our passage where we're told that 'all the Athenians and the foreigners who lived there spent their time doing nothing but talking about and listening to the latest ideas.' When Paul went to Athens, then, he was going into the world of philosophy and philosophers. Athens had been the city of philosophers for centuries. Several hundred years before Christ was born, Athens was home to three of the greatest philosophers who have ever lived: Socrates, Plato and Aristotle. Plato founded his 'Academy' in Athens, the forerunner of the modern university. Aristotle was a student at the Academy but then went on to found his 'Lyceum' as a rival college. At the time Paul went to visit Athens, as described in our passage, it was still the centre for Greek philosophy, although Plato and Aristotle had given way to Epicurean and Stoic philosophy. It was, in fact, a group of Epicurean and Stoic philosophers who confronted Paul in Athens.

Up until this point, Paul had been speaking about Christ both to Jews and Greeks. In verse 17 we read that he 'reasoned in the synagogue with the Jews and the God-fearing Greeks, as well as in the market place day by day with those who happened to be there.' That is to say, Paul was preaching the good news about Jesus Christ to anyone who would listen. Now in a city which, as we have seen, loved listening to new ideas, it was inevitable that Paul would soon come to the attention of those who liked new ideas. These Epicurean and Stoic philosophers first of all began to argue with him (verse 18) and then took him to a meeting of the Areopagus (verse 19). The Areopagus was an ancient institution, a kind of court which had considerable authority in religious matters. It was possible for visiting teachers to be brought before the Areopagus to give an account of their teaching and that is what Paul was required to do.

Athens was also a centre for religions of various kinds and Paul had been greatly disturbed when he had first arrived in Athens to see the many idols representing various gods. This provided him with an opening in his conversation with the philosophers: 'Paul then stood up in the meeting of the Areopagus and said: "Men of Athens! I see that in every way you are very religious. For as I walked around and looked carefully at your objects of worship, I even found an altar with this inscription: TO AN UNKNOWN GOD. Now what you worship as something unknown I am going to proclaim to you' (Acts 17:22–23).

The Athenians had many gods and each god had an idol or a number of idols but just to make sure that they had covered every eventuality, they even had an idol to the 'unknown god'! This gave Paul an opportunity to speak of the living God who is not an idol made of wood or stone and does not live in a temple or any other kind of building but rather is the one who made everything that exists, as the Creator. This God, says Paul, gives life to all human beings and he himself decided where they would live and so on.

As Paul went on to explain, each human being must one day come to terms with this God since they will certainly face him on the Day of Judgement. He spelled out to the Athenians that God has set aside a day when he will judge the world with justice through Jesus Christ. The proof that this is going to happen, says Paul, is the fact that God has raised Jesus Christ from the dead. As soon as Paul mentioned the resurrection, we're told (verse 32) that some of them 'sneered'. The idea of resurrection did not fit in with their philosophy and so they could not accept it. They were interested in some of Paul's new ideas and might well have been happy to add some of his ideas to theirs but they were not prepared to throw out their own ideas altogether and begin again, yet that is precisely what Paul wanted them to do. He did not want them to add the God and Father of our Lord Jesus Christ to the list of idols; he wanted them to abandon all their idols and worship the one true and living God. He was clear that Christianity cannot cohabit with other religions and philosophies. It claims to be the one unique way to God and the evidence for that claim is the resurrection of Jesus Christ from the dead. He was effectively telling them that they could accept or reject Christianity but they could not mix and match it with other philosophies or religions.

One of the great concerns of some of the early Christian theologians was that people were trying to take pagan philosophy and add Christianity on as an extra on top. It was the great theologian Tertullian who warned against this danger and said, 'What indeed has Jerusalem to do with Athens? What concord is there between the Academy and the Church?' The point he was making is that Christianity cannot be built on the foundation of pagan philosophy. Throughout the centuries people have tried to build a Christian theology on the foundation of philosophy. In the mediaeval period Aristotle provided the foundation. At the time of the Enlightenment in the eighteenth century, Immanuel Kant provided the foundation. In the twentieth century attempts were made to build a theology on the foundation of existentialist philosophy. All these attempts failed because a truly Christian theology can only be built on the foundation of a truly Christian philosophy (or worldview). In other words, we must get our philosophy as well as our theology from the Bible. The uniqueness of Christ is such that the truth about him cannot be built on any foundation other than God's revelation itself.

Cornelius Van Til spent his entire life trying to convey this message about the need for a Christian philosophy upon which to build a Christian theology. He also showed very clearly the dangers of building theology on the foundation of secular philosophy. As he demonstrated, the reason why many theologians deny the miracles or the uniqueness of Christ or the incarnation or the infallibility of Scripture is because they bring to the Bible a series of presuppositions which have come from their philosophy and they allow these presuppositions to determine their attitude to miracles and Scripture and so on. When scholars came to write a book in honour of Van Til's seventy-fifth birthday, they called it *Jerusalem and Athens*!

Conclusion

The first Christians lived in a multicultural society with many religions but they would not be moved from their conviction that Jesus Christ was unique. They refused to put Jesus on the same level as anyone else. Peter and John insisted on their right to proclaim the uniqueness of Christ and were prepared to challenge the ruling authorities and, if necessary, to disobey them. Paul went to Athens where there were many gods but he did not add his God to the list of deities. He challenged the Athenians, arguing that there was only one God and that they must look to him for meaning, purpose and salvation.

We are being told today that because we live in a multicultural society we have no right to make claims to uniqueness but we must resist these voices. Evangelicals have faced up to Liberal Theology for over 250 years and there is good reason to think that we are beginning to win the battle. There are more evangelical scholars and evangelical theological colleges than ever before; and the number of those who call themselves 'evangelicals' has increased to such an extent that we represent one of the most significant segments of the world-wide church. Our scholars have written books and answered the liberals and the tide has begun to turn. Above all, the intellectual bankruptcy of liberalism has been apparent to all.

The problem is that the situation has now changed, with the advent of pluralism. Before, we were fighting on one front, the battle for the authority of the Bible as God's infallible Word. Now we are being called to fight on another front, the battle for the uniqueness of Christ. It is no coincidence that the battles which we have to wage are centred on these two key elements of the Christian faith because our enemy the devil knows what he is doing. If you can persuade people that the Bible is not the Word of God and if you can persuade people that Jesus Christ is *not* uniquely the Son of God and the only way to God, then Christianity is finished.

The greatest danger facing the Christian church today is the temptation to compromise on the uniqueness of Christ. As Christians, we must identify and oppose the dangers of liberalism and pluralism. We must not ignore the fact that the world church has been affected by these views, nor can we ignore the fact that many so-called Christians have found teachers who will say the things they want to hear. We cannot retreat into the ghetto or into the safety of supposedly doctrinally pure churches. We must communicate this gospel, we must correct, rebuke and encourage and we must challenge the forces which deny the uniqueness of Christ. We must not fail to take up this challenge.

The Author:

The Rev. Professor A.T.B. McGowan is minister of Inverness East Church of Scotland and professor of theology in the University of the Highlands and Islands. He is honorary professor in Reformed doctrine in the University of Aberdeen and chairman of the Theological Commission of the World Reformed Fellowship. He is also president of the Scottish Evangelical Theology Society. Professor McGowan is married to June and they have three sons.

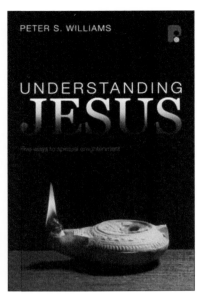

Understanding Jesus

Five Ways to Spiritual Enlightenment

Peter Williams

Peter Williams examines the Gospel accounts of Jesus' life from an apologetic perspective clearing the ground from pre-conceived ideas and prejudices and opening up five ways to consider the claims of Jesus' life and ministry. Williams encourages readers to take Jesus seriously and gives serious reasons why we should. Understanding Jesus helps readers to make their own informed response to the historical Jesus.

> 'Aquinas offered five ways to God; Peter Williams gives five powerful reasons for thinking that God revealed Himself in Jesus Christ. While the new atheists recycle nineteenth century doubts about the historicity and divinity of Jesus, Williams appeals to the most recent work of qualified scholars, including secularists and Jewish scholars as well as Christian authorities. He shows the evidence is stronger than ever for the New Testament account of Jesus' life and works, and that Jesus continues to transform lives today – **Angus J. L. Menuge Ph.D., Professor of Philosophy, Concordia University Wisconsin, USA.**

Peter S. Williams is a Christian philosopher and apologist. He is an Assistant Professor in Communication & Worldviews, Gimlekollen School of Journalism and Communication, Kristiansand, Norway.

978-1-84227-739-3

Paternoster:
thinking faith

We trust you enjoyed reading this book from Paternoster. If you want to be informed of any new titles from this author and other releases you can sign up to the Paternoster newsletter by contacting us:

Contact us
By Post: Paternoster
52 Presley Way
Crownhill
Milton Keynes
MK8 0ES

E-mail:paternoster@authenticmedia.co.uk

Follow us:

ND - #0167 - 090625 - C0 - 229/152/13 - PB - 9781842277492 - Gloss Lamination